KEATS'S
SHAKESPEARE

Oxford University Press, Ely House, London W.1

GLASGOW NEW YORK TORONTO MELBOURNE WELLINGTON
CAPE TOWN SALISBURY IBADAN NAIROBI LUSAKA ADDIS ABABA
BOMBAY CALCUTTA MADRAS KARACHI LAHORE DACCA
KUALA LUMPUR HONG KONG TOKYO

FIRST PUBLISHED 1928
REPRINTED LITHOGRAPHICALLY IN GREAT BRITAIN
AT THE UNIVERSITY PRESS, OXFORD
BY VIVIAN RIDLER
PRINTER TO THE UNIVERSITY
1966

SKETCH OF KEATS BY JOSEPH SEVERN
done on board the *Maria Crowther*, September 1820
From the original water-colour drawing in the possession of the author

' *the fire is at its last click—I am sitting with my back to it
with one foot rather askew upon the rug and the other with the
heel a little elevated from the carpet—I am writing this on the
Maid's tragedy which I have read since tea with Great pleasure. . . .*

*These are trifles but I require nothing so much of you but that
you will give me a like description of yourselves, however it may
be when you are writing to me. Could I see the same thing done
of any great Man long since dead it would be a great delight : As
to know in what position Shakespeare sat when he began " To be
or not to be "—such things become interesting from distance of
time or place.'*

*Written on March 12th, 1819, in the journal letter to George
and Georgiana Keats, begun Feb. 24th, 1819.*

KEATS'S SHAKESPEARE

A DESCRIPTIVE STUDY

BY

CAROLINE F. E. SPURGEON

OXFORD
AT THE CLARENDON PRESS

I never quite despair and I read Shakespeare—indeed I shall I think never read any other Book much . . . I am very near agreeing with Hazlitt that Shakespeare is enough for us.

Letter to Haydon, from Margate, 10th May 1817.

I have great reason to be content, for thank God I can read, and perhaps understand Shakespeare to his depths.

Letter to John Taylor, from Hampstead, 27th February 1818.

I have enjoyed Shakespeare more with Keats than with any other human creature.

Haydon's *Journal,* March 1821, in *Memoirs of Haydon,* by Tom Taylor, 1853, vol. ii, p. 8.

Things real, such as existences of Sun, moon, and Stars— and passages of Shakespeare.

Letter to Bailey, from Teignmouth, 13th March 1818.

Shakspeare and the Paradise lost every day become greater wonders to me. I look upon fine phrases like a lover.

Letter to Bailey, from Winchester, 15th August 1819.

The best sort of Poetry—that is all I care for, all I live for.

Letter to Reynolds, from Winchester, 25th August 1819.

FOREWORD

LOVERS of poetry will readily imagine what would be their sensations were they unexpectedly to come across a copy, say, of Ovid's *Metamorphoses* with Shakespeare's undoubted autograph on the title-page and with underlinings and annotations by him scattered over the whole book; such a discovery it will be said is just the kind of golden day-dream which none but a foolish book-lover could have.

Something akin to these sensations were, however, actually mine on the day a few months ago when, quite unexpectedly, I found myself handling Keats's own edition of Shakespeare, with his own name on the title-page, and the whole book scored, marked, and annotated by him.

This happy discovery came about thus.

I was spending a radiant October week-end with some friends in the wooded highlands near New York, and another visitor, hearing I was interested in such things, asked me rather tentatively whether I would care to look at a copy of Shakespeare which had some marks in it by Keats, and which belonged to a friend of hers who lived at Princeton. She had not seen it for a good many years, but she rather thought or conveyed the idea to me that it had belonged to Joseph Severn, and that Keats had been reading it in Rome and had left some markings in it.

Even that of course was enough for me; I would gladly have gone to California to have a look at it; and the matter was most kindly arranged, so that a few weeks later I found myself one fine morning in Mr. George Armour's beautiful library in Princeton, with my host smilingly handing to me seven rather shabby little volumes. On opening the first one I found at once to my astonishment and delight that this was Keats's own Shakespeare, the book he had read and re-read and marked and annotated during the last three and a half years of his life.

I had not expected this, because I could not have believed that the existence of this important and interesting book in so accessible a place could for so long have remained unnoticed.

It was a strange and moving experience when I actually held in my hand these little volumes, which for years had been Keats's cherished companions, and eagerly looked through the pages which bear such clear marks of their owner's delight and admiration, as well as of his close, acute attention to word and phrase. They seemed to me so full of interest for all students of Keats as well as of Shakespeare, that I asked Mr. Armour's permission, which he most kindly gave me, to write a description of them, to reproduce some of their pages, and to print a considerable proportion of the marked passages.

I should like to record here my most grateful thanks to Mr. Armour, in which I am sure all Keats lovers will join, for this ready and generous permission, and for having made everything so easy for my somewhat lengthy and detailed study.

Miss Amy Lowell had not my good fortune in having access to the books, nor does she mention their existence in her *Life of Keats*; indeed, I understand from Mr. Armour that no specialist student of English has examined them during the forty-seven years they have been in his possession until I was privileged to do so the other day.

We know now for certain that Keats owned and marked in all nine volumes of Shakespeare; these seven of what we may call the ' Princeton copy ', the 1808 reprint of the folio edition of 1623, and the volume of Shakespeare's *Poems*, which last two books are now in the Dilke Collection at Hampstead.

For the convenience of readers I have included in this study of the Princeton copy some account of the marks and annotations in the volumes at Hampstead, as well as a complete reprint of Keats's markings of *Troilus and Cressida* in the folio edition. For permission to do this I desire to thank the Hampstead Public Libraries Committee.

This book gives therefore a fairly comprehensive description, and in part a reproduction, of the marks and annotations made by Keats in the whole of his reading of Shakespeare. It thus forms an authentic record of the study and the love of our greatest poet by the one whom many to-day place nearest to him, and as such I believe it cannot fail to be of interest and value to all who care for English letters.

The water-colour sketch of Keats which is reproduced in facsimile for the frontispiece is attributed to Joseph Severn, and is said to have been done on the *Maria Crowther* on the voyage to Naples in September 1820. It appears as if Keats were sitting in some kind of deck chair in the open air, for he is in a heavy overcoat and his hair is ruffled. It is noticeable how ill and hollow-cheeked he looks, and one is reminded in what strong terms Severn expresses concern at his changed appearance two months earlier, when writing to Haslam in July 1820.

Mr. Arthur Severn, who has examined the sketch, confirms it as being his father's work, and agrees with me that it is clearly done from life.

It will be noted that it has a marked resemblance to Severn's posthumous portrait of Keats reading, now in the National Portrait Gallery, and reproduced by Colvin in his *Life*, to face p. 338.

Both these portraits are noticeably unlike the three earlier ones—the pencil sketch by Charles Brown, drawn at Shanklin in the summer of 1819, and the two silhouettes, probably both by Brown. All three of these are reproduced by Amy Lowell in her *Life*, vol. ii, frontispiece, and to face p. 268. They all three alike have curly hair and the nose slightly tip-tilted.

On the other hand, the life-mask has a straight rather long nose, very much like that in this portrait and in the posthumous one by Severn. In both of these latter the hair is straight and rather lank. Possibly illness affected Keats's hair, and thinned and straightened it.

The history of the sketch here reproduced and published for the first time is obscure. All that I have as yet ascertained for certain is that it was in the possession of Mr. Eustace Conway of New York, from whom it came over to London recently, and was sold at Sotheby's on July the 27th, 1928, when I bought it.

Mr. Arthur Severn definitely says it is not the sketch done by his father which was 'removed' many years ago from his scrap-book. That was a highly finished, careful pencil drawing of Keats lying reading in his berth, the shape of which Mr. Severn has sketched in a letter to me thus:

So that the water-colour sketch here reproduced as the frontispiece, is clearly yet another drawing of Severn's hitherto unknown to the general public.

It is a happy coincidence that enables me to combine with the account of the equally unknown Shakespeare volumes, this new glimpse of how Keats sometimes looked when he sat absorbed in reading them.

CAROLINE F. E. SPURGEON.

ALCISTON, SUSSEX,
August 1928.

KEATS'S SHAKESPEARE

IT has generally been assumed that in addition to the 1808 reprint
of the 1623 folio edition, and the volume of Shakespeare's *Poems*
given him by Reynolds, both now in the Dilke Collection at Hampstead, Keats possessed another copy of Shakespeare; and in con-
firmation of this a seven-volume edition, 12mo, bound, is among
the list of Keats's books drawn up by Richard Woodhouse,[1] with
the note that the sixth volume is lost.

Mr. Buxton Forman twice refers to the existence of this book,
and describes it as a 'Johnson and Steevens's edition of Shakespeare'
which at Keats's death passed into the hands of Severn. In the
latest written note (1901) he says, 'The book was of considerable
interest, being, it is said, annotated by Keats in manuscript. At
Severn's death it passed to his medical attendant, a Dr. Valeriani
of Rome; and when he in turn was gathered to his fathers, it was
purchased and re-sold for export to America. I did not see it, and
do not know its present resting place.'[2]

For nearly fifty years this book had been lost sight of, until by
a happy chance I came across it in America last autumn in the way
I have described in the Foreword.

The lost sixth volume must fortunately have been found after
Woodhouse made his list, for the edition is now complete,
and consists of a set of seven stocky and rather attractive little
volumes, chosen, one would imagine, chiefly for their handy pocket
size ($4\frac{3}{4}'' \times 3''$); well-printed little books with woodcut illustrations,
published by Whittingham at Chiswick in 1814.

They have been re-bound, probably for Severn in Rome,[3] as
their coats are now of the white vellum so usual in Italy, with plain

---

[1] Now in the Morgan Library, New York; printed by Sidney Colvin, *Life of Keats*,
1917, pp. 556–8.
[2] Note in *The Complete Works of John Keats*, ed. by H. Buxton Forman, 5 vols., 1901,
vol. iii, p. 245; and prefixed to the Notes on Shakespeare in *The Poetical Works and other
Writings of John Keats*, edited by Harry Buxton Forman, 4 vols., 1883, vol. iii, p. 2.
[3] Their present binding is of exactly the same type as that of the volume of Shakespeare's

gold tooling; I regret to say that in re-binding they have been ' barbarously cropped ', so that in one case at least Keats's notes are not easily legible.

The history of the book is simple. Keats had it with him in Rome, and, before the end, gave it to Severn, for on the title-page of the first volume he has added after his own name the words 'to Joseph Severn' (see Plate 1). Severn spent a large part of his long life in Rome, where in 1879 he died, and these little volumes were bought in the spring of 1881, at the sale of some of Keats's manuscripts and other relics which had belonged to Severn, by Mr. George Armour of Princeton, in whose possession they still are.[1]

Keats, who has written his name in the first two volumes—'John Keats, April 1817'—must have bought the books in London just before going off alone to the Isle of Wight for quiet and study, which he did on Monday, April the 14th, of that year.. We know he left the Bull and Crown Inn, Holborn, at half-past seven on that evening, travelled all night on the stage coach, 'three stages outside and the rest in for it began to be very cold', and almost immediately after his arrival at the inn at Southampton, evidently already feeling homesick, he sat down to write to his brothers. ' I felt rather lonely this Morning at breakfast,' he says, 'so I went and unbox'd a Shakspeare—"There's my Comfort".' This then is the actual book— a new and treasured possession—which he unpacked on that April morning a hundred and eleven years ago, and I imagine it was the first volume, now so much marked, which he read, and that probably he slipped it into his pocket when he went out after breakfast to Southampton Water to inquire at what time the boat started to the Isle of Wight.

Keats, naturally, had known and cared for Shakespeare from his

Poems, annotated by Keats, which he also gave to Severn, and which is now in the Dilke Collection at the Hampstead Public Library. Doubtless they were re-bound by the same hand.

[1] It is possible that between the date of Severn's death and the sale of his possessions the books may, as Mr. Buxton Forman says, have passed to Dr. Valeriani of Rome; but it is certain that they were sold in London by Messrs. H. Sotheran & Co. with other Keats relics belonging to Severn in 1881, when Mr. Armour bought them; see the Athenaeum, 2nd April 1881, p. 461.

PLATE I

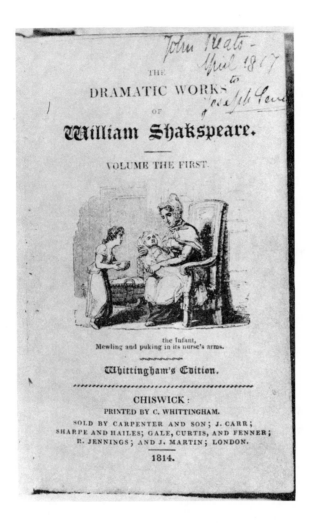

Title-page of the first volume of *Keats's Shakespeare*

schooldays; Cowden Clarke tells of his coming over to the old school from Edmonton when he was probably about sixteen, and, while reading *Cymbeline* aloud, being profoundly moved at the passage where Imogen says she would have watched Posthumus and followed him

> till he had melted from
> The smallness of a gnat to air.

But, although he had read him, he had not 'felt him to the full',[1] he had not given himself up to him, until this spring of 1817, half way through his twenty-second year, when suddenly, as it seemed, his mind and imagination became literally aflame with Shakespeare.

It was the moment of rallying his forces between his first two great creative efforts, the *Poems* of 1817 and *Endymion*, and it would seem as if he had turned instinctively to Shakespeare for inspiration and support. He read him, marked him, quoted him, and parodied him; thought of him, brooded over him, steeped himself in him; the music of his lines haunted him, stimulated him to write, sustained and delighted him. He finds a head of Shakespeare in his lodgings at Carisbrooke and hangs it over his books, 'this alone is a good morning's work'; he is clearly pleased and thinks it 'ominous of good' when his kindly landlady insists that he shall take it with him 'though I went away in a hurry'; he begs Reynolds whenever he writes to say a word or two on some passage in Shakespeare that has particularly struck him; he writes to Haydon (10th May 1817), 'I remember your saying that you had notions of a good Genius presiding over you. I have of late had the same thought, for things which [I] do half at Random are afterwards confirmed by my judgment in a dozen features of Propriety. Is it too daring to fancy Shakespeare this Presider?'

It is a little later in the same letter, which is full of Shakespeare, beginning with *Love's Labour's Lost* and ending with *Antony and Cleopatra*, that he says, 'I never quite despair and I read Shakespeare —indeed I shall I think never read any other Book much . . . I

---

1 'We read fine things, but never feel them to the full until we have gone the same steps as the author', in the famous and amazingly profound letter to Reynolds of 3rd May 1818.

am very near agreeing with Hazlitt that Shakespeare is enough for us.'

And at the end of 1817, this shaping year of his poetic life, he records [1] that he has arrived at the realization of two fundamental truths about Shakespeare, truths which were profoundly to influence his own work and being, for Shakespeare was to him from then on a touchstone and a beacon, the ideal man of genius and poet.

The first is the intensity of Shakespeare's art, which causes 'all disagreeables' to 'evaporate from their being in close relationship with Beauty and Truth', and the second is the 'Negative Capability' of his character, 'that is, when a man is capable of being in uncertainties, mysteries, doubts, without any irritable reaching after fact and reason'. It was through and with Shakespeare, during this year of miraculous growth, that Keats gradually found his way to his own deepest and most original convictions about life and poetry, to the realization that great poetry is the outcome of great living, the secret of which is a seeking of, a reception of, and a submission to experience—'nothing ever becomes real till it is experienced', 'until we are sick we understand not'—and further and consequently that 'a fine writer is the most genuine being in the world'.[2]

To return to April and May of the year 1817, and Keats's new volumes of Shakespeare.

The five letters that we have of his during these two months, all most interesting—to his brothers, to Reynolds, to Leigh Hunt, to Haydon, and to his new publishers, Taylor and Hessey—are all alike saturated in Shakespearian thought, and it is worth noting that of the fifteen Shakespearian allusions or quotations in these five letters, six are to *The Tempest*, the first play in volume one, which is freely marked and clearly much read, and five of the others are to plays in the first two volumes, which are those, I believe, he was reading very specially at this time.

One of the significant and new facts which these books reveal is

---

[1] In the short but most remarkable letter to his brothers of 28th Dec. 1817.

[2] For the development and exposition of what these truths, discovered through and with Shakespeare, meant to Keats's spirit and art, all lovers of both poets are deeply in the debt of Mr. Middleton Murry, *Keats and Shakespeare*, 1925.

PLATE 2

Ajax. A whoreson dog, that shall palter thus with us!
I would, he were a Trojan!
    Nest.   What a vice
Were it in Ajax now——
    Ulyss.   If he were proud?
    Dio. Or covetous of praise?
    Ulyss.   Ay, or surly borne?
    Dio. Or strange, or self-affected?
    Ulyss. Thank the heavens, lord, thou art of sweet
        composure;
Praise him that got thee, she that gave thee suck:
Fam'd be thy tutor, and thy parts of nature
Thrice-fam'd, beyond all erudition:
But he that disciplin'd thy arms to fight,
Let Mars divide eternity in twain,
And give him half: and, for thy vigour,
Bull-bearing Milo his addition yield
To sinewy Ajax. I'll not praise thy wisdom,
Which, like a bourn, a pale, a shore, confines
Thy spacious and dilated parts: Here's Nestor,—
Instructed by the antiquary times,
He must, he is, he cannot but be wise:—
But pardon, father Nestor, were your days
As green as Ajax', and your brain so temper'd,
You should not have the eminence of him,
But be as Ajax.
    Ajax.   Shall I call you father?
    Nest. Ay, my good son.
    Dio.   Be rul'd by him, lord Ajax.
    Ulyss. There is no tarrying here; the hart Achilles
Keeps thicket. Please it our great general
To call together all his state of war;
Fresh kings are come to Troy: To-morrow,
We must with all our main of power stand fast:
And here's a lord,—come knights from east to west,
And cull their flower, Ajax shall cope the best.
    Agam. Go we to council. Let Achilles sleep:
Light boats sail swift, though greater hulks draw deep.
                    [*Exeunt.*

A page from *Troilus and Cressida*, a play
showing no signs of having been read in this
edition

Compare it with pages from The Tempest, A Midsummer Night's
Dream, *and* Antony and Cleopatra, *plates* 3, 4, *and* 11

which plays Keats read and marked most. Quite apart from the marking, it is clear from the look and feel of the paper which plays have been most constantly read. This can be seen even in the photograph; compare, for instance, the sharp edge of the paper and clean crisp appearance of a page from *Troilus and Cressida* (Plate 2), a play not read by Keats in this edition, with the edges and texture of the page in *The Tempest* (Plate 3), *A Midsummer Night's Dream* (Plate 4) or in *Antony and Cleopatra* (Plate 11).

If we add to the testimony of these volumes the markings in his folio edition of Shakespeare and in his copy of the *Poems*, of which an account is given later (see p. 38 below), we have a fairly full and reliable record of Keats's reading of Shakespeare.

In the seven volumes of the Princeton copy both the marking and the wear of the paper clearly prove that *The Tempest* and *A Midsummer Night's Dream* were by far the most read; next, and approximately in this order, *Measure for Measure, Antony and Cleopatra, The Merchant of Venice, Cymbeline,* and *A Winter's Tale.* Volume vii, which contains *Pericles, King Lear, Romeo and Juliet, Hamlet,* and *Othello,* compared with volume i, is little marked but has been a great deal read, especially *Romeo and Juliet, King Lear,* and *Othello,* all entirely unmarked; of these three the first appears to have been the most read.

Hamlet is a good deal underlined, and *Pericles,* though it has only one mark, the underlining of 'In the day's glorious walk' (I. ii. 4), has been well read.

The remaining plays in the first two volumes, *Two Gentlemen, Twelfth Night, Much Ado, As You Like It,* and *All's Well,* have been a good deal read and have all some markings; indeed, the only plays in these two volumes which have not been much read are the *Merry Wives* and *Love's Labour's Lost.*

Other plays which are noticeably little read in this edition are the *Comedy of Errors* (hardly marked, save for two lines in Ægeon's speech, V. i. 310, 312), *Troilus and Cressida* (unmarked), *Timon* (unmarked), *Taming of the Shrew* ('Adonis painted by a running brook' and the following three lines, Induction ii. 52–5, are the only marks), *King John, Richard II, Henry V*, and the three parts of *Henry VI*, which latter look as if they had not been read at all. But we know, for Keats tells us so, that he read them later in the year (Dec. 1817) and clearly read them with great care, when preparing to write his review of Kean in *Richard Duke of York*, a play compiled from the three parts of *Henry VI*. The puzzle is in what copy of Shakespeare he read them, for in his folio edition, as in these volumes, the pages of these plays look noticeably fresh and unread.

There are no marks, underlinings, or annotations in any one of the historical plays, but the two parts of *Henry IV* (especially the second part), *Richard III*, and *Henry VIII* have been read to some extent. *Coriolanus* and *Julius Caesar* also are unmarked, but have both been read.

All this is very much what we should expect. Keats was reading, especially in 1817, chiefly for poetry of the more 'romantic' kind, and was peculiarly attracted, as we can tell from what he underlines, by epithets and imagery; and it is natural, therefore, that *The Tempest, A Midsummer Night's Dream*, and *Romeo and Juliet* should be favourites.

We are not really left in any doubt about the matter, for he himself has admirably expressed his attitude to the historical plays in the review already referred to, which appeared in *The Champion* for Sunday, 28th Dec. 1817. In the course of this he says:

'They (the historical dramas) are written with infinite vigour, but their regularity tied the hand of Shakespeare. Particular facts kept him in the high road, and would not suffer him to turn down leafy and winding lanes, or to break wildly and at once into the breathing fields. The poetry is for the most part ironed and manacled with a chain of facts, and cannot get free; it cannot escape from the prison house of history, nor often move without our being disturbed with the clanking of its fetters. The poetry of Shakespeare is generally free as is the wind—a perfect thing of the elements, winged and sweetly coloured. Poetry must be free! It is of the air, not of the earth; and the higher it soars the nearer it gets to its home. The poetry of "Romeo and Juliet",

PLATE 3

A freckled whelp, hag-born,) not honour'd with
A human shape.

Ari. Yes; Caliban, her son.

Pro. Dull thing, I say so; he, that Caliban,
Whom now I keep in service. Thou best know'st
What torment I did find thee in: thy groans
Did make wolves howl, and penetrate the breasts
Of ever-angry bears: it was a torment
To lay upon the damn'd, which Sycorax
Could not again undo; it was mine art,
When I arriv'd, and heard thee, that made gape
The pine, and let thee out.

Ari. I thank thee, master.

Pro. If thou more murmur'st, I will rend an oak,
And peg thee in his knotty entrails, till
Thou hast howl'd away twelve winters.

Ari. Pardon, master:
I will be correspondent to command,
And do my spiriting gently.

Pro. Do so; and after two days
I will discharge thee.

Ari. That's my noble master!
What shall I do? say what: what shall I do?

Pro. Go make thyself like to a nymph o'the sea;
Be subject to no sight but mine; invisible
To every eye-ball else. Go, take this shape,
And hither come in't: hence, with diligence. [*Exit Ariel.*

Awake, dear heart, awake! thou hast slept well;
Awake!

Mira. The strangeness of your story put
Heaviness in me.

Pro. Shake it off: come on;
We'll visit Caliban, my slave, who never
Yields us kind answer.

Mira. 'Tis a villain, sir,
I do not love to look on.

Pro. But, as 'tis,
We cannot miss him: he does make our fire,
Fetch in our wood; and serves in offices
That profit us. What, ho! slave! Caliban!

Thou earth, thou! speak.

Cal. [*Within.*] There's wood enough within.

Pro. Come forth, I say; there's other business for thee;
Come forth, thou tortoise! when?

Re-enter ARIEL, *like a Water-Nymph.*

Fine apparition! My quaint Ariel,
Hark in thine ear.

Ari. My lord, it shall be done. [*Exit.*

Pro. Thou poisonous slave, got by the devil himself
Upon thy wicked dam, come forth!

Enter CALIBAN.

Cal. As wicked dew as e'er my mother brush'd
With raven's feather from unwholesome fen,
Drop on you both! a south-west blow on ye,
And blister you all o'er!

Pro. For this, be sure, to-night thou shalt have cramps,
Side-stitches, that shall pen thy breath up; urchins
Shall, for that vast of night that they may work,
All exercise on thee: thou shalt be pinch'd
As thick as honeycombs, each pinch more stinging
Than bees that made them.

Cal. I must eat my dinner.
This island's mine, by Sycorax, my mother,
Which thou tak'st from me. When thou camest first,
Thou strok'dst me, and mad'st much of me; would'st
Water with berries in't; and teach me how [give me
To name the bigger light, and how the less,
That burn by day and night: and then I lov'd thee,
And show'd thee all the qualities o'the isle,
The fresh springs, brine pits, barren place, and fertile;
Cursed be I that did so!——All the charms
Of Sycorax, toads, beetles, bats, light on you!
For I am all the subjects that you have,
Which first was mine own king; and here you sty me
In this hard rock, whiles you do keep from me
The rest of the island.

Pro. Thou most lying slave,
Whom stripes may move, not kindness; I have us'd thee,
Filth as thou art, with human care; and lodg'd thee
In mine own cell, till thou didst seek to violate

A much read and marked page in *The Tempest*

Note the signs of use and thumb marks on the right-hand page

of "Hamlet", of "Macbeth", is the poetry of Shakespeare's soul—full of love and divine romance. It knows no stop in its delight, but "goeth where it listeth"—remaining, however, in all men's hearts a perpetual and golden dream. The poetry of "Lear", "Othello", "Cymbeline", etc., is the poetry of human passions and affections, made almost ethereal by the power of the poet. Again, the poetry of "Richard", "John", and the Henries is the blending [of] the imaginative with the historical: it is poetry!—but oftentimes poetry wandering on the London Road.'

Of the three kinds of poetry here so acutely described, that which called most irresistibly to Keats in that spring of 1817, when, I feel sure, most of the underlining was done in these volumes, was 'the poetry of Shakespeare's soul—full of love and divine romance'.

I have here reproduced (see pp. 66–148 below) all underlinings and annotations in the four plays most marked by Keats in this edition, *The Tempest*, *A Midsummer Night's Dream*, *Measure for Measure*, and *Antony and Cleopatra*.

With the first of these to refer to, we may for a moment look over Keats's shoulder as, sitting in his Carisbrooke lodgings or later at Margate, he marks and underlines *The Tempest*, and see what light these markings throw on what arrests and enchants him.

As we should expect, he has marked most of the long speeches; those which are vividly descriptive, such as Ariel's account of his activities when he 'flamed amazement' on the ship (I. ii. 196–206) or Prospero's reminder to Ariel of his sufferings from Sycorax (I. ii. 272–83), Caliban's curses on Prospero (I. ii. 321–44 and II. ii. 1–14), and Ariel's enchanting picture of the three men of sin 'like unbacked colts' pricking their ears and calf-like following his tabor into the 'filthy mantled pool' (IV. i. 172–81); and those which are exquisitely beautiful, steeped in music and colour, such as 'Be not afeard, the isle is full of noises' (III. ii. 147–55), which is trebly marked, underlined, and with two lines down the side as well; Iris's greeting to Ceres and her reply (IV. i. 60–71, 78–83), 'You sunburnt sicklemen' (IV. i. 134–8), and Prospero's two great speeches (IV. i. 148–63; V. i. 33–48).

What strikes us, however, as perhaps unusual in looking through these markings is Keats's sensitive appreciation of the elaborate and peculiarly beautiful stage directions. He underlines nearly all of them—the strange Shapes, bringing in a banquet, who 'dance about it with gentle Actions of Salutation', and when they re-enter, 'dance with Mops and Mowes', the description of the dance of the Reapers and the Nymphs in Act IV, and its sudden ending, or the very full and charming direction in Act V, a little drama in itself:

'Solemn music. Re-enter Ariel: after him, Alonso, with a 'frantic Gesture, attended by Gonzalo; Sebastian and Antonio 'in like manner, attended by Adrian and Francisco: They all 'enter the Circle which Prospero had made, and there stand 'charmed: which Prospero observing, speaks.'

Further, we note his intense interest in Ariel, his different appearances, his characteristics, his elemental nature, and association with music. He is naturally enchanted with his songs, especially the first four lines of

Come unto these yellow sands,

he marks many of his speeches, often doubly or even trebly (as I. ii. 190–3, 222–4), while the promise to 'do my spiriting gently' (I. ii. 298) has three side-marks in addition to the underlining.

He underlines all Prospero's epithets and methods of addressing him: 'my Ariel', 'my brave spirit', 'Dull thing', 'my quaint Ariel', 'delicate Ariel', 'fine Ariel', 'my dainty Ariel', 'my tricksy spirit', 'my diligence', 'my Ariel chick'; he notes every touch which throws light on his character, nature, or appearance, as his account of his 'worthy service' to Prospero (I. ii. 247–9), his master's assurance that he shall 'be free as mountain winds', his description of him, 'thou which art but air', Ferdinand's comment on his song, 'This is no mortal business', Ariel's exclamations, 'I drink the air before me', and 'all afire with me', and finally Prospero's valediction (marked thrice at the sides as well as underlined)

to the elements
Be free, and fare thou well!

He is concerned not only with his nature and temperament, but also with his appearance, and is evidently following the staging with the closest attention, noting (i.e. underlining) nearly all the stage directions dealing with him; when he is invisible, or if visible, what he is doing, what characters he assumes, and the part that music and other sounds play throughout.

Caliban also attracts him greatly—his nature, his curses, his language.

We must remember that during these months of April and May 1817, when Keats was saturating himself in Shakespeare and especially in *The Tempest*, his mind and imagination were aflame with his own great conception, his new poem, which he certainly had already shaped and planned, and which he probably began writing some time during the third week in April. In the light of this it is clear that the great interest shown in Ariel and Caliban, creatures of the air and of the earth and water, is closely connected with the ideas which were then thronging in his head so that he could not sleep o' nights, of the scenery and adventures of Endymion and of the great hymn to Pan, the god who keeps away the very infections and mildews with which Caliban curses Prospero,

> Breather round our farms,
> To keep off mildews, and all weather harms:

and who, like Ariel, is a

> Strange ministrant of undescribed sounds,
> That come a-swooning over hollow grounds.[1]

With this clue, one cannot look through the underlined passages in the play, and the first two books of *Endymion* especially, and not be convinced that the atmosphere and descriptions which excited and delighted him in *The Tempest* blended with, and in this early part sometimes overshadowed, other suggestions and influences to a far greater extent than has hitherto been recognized. It becomes

[1] I do not forget that strange sounds and mysterious flutings are always attributed to Pan, and that Keats would read that this is so in Baldwin's (William Godwin's) *Pantheon*, which we know he possessed. But *The Tempest* influence, because more poetical and imaginative, was probably the more potent.

clear that the early part of Keats's poem is literally steeped in the atmosphere of nature spirits, invisible music, green verdure, 'lush and lusty grass', and visions of colour, beauty, and magic which have specially entranced him in Shakespeare's play.

Intermittent music, elusive, alluring, exquisite, haunts us through both poems. The 'quick invisible strings' of Peona's lute, the 'swift treble pipe and humming string', the 'dew-dropping melody' heard by Endymion, which

> came more softly than the east could blow
> Arion's magic to the Atlantic isles,

these are closely akin to the 'solemn, strange', and 'marvellous sweet' airs of Prospero's island.

The masque of Iris and Ceres, with its rich nature poetry, clearly delights him, and we are reminded of it when we read of the sheep nibbling 'their fill at ocean's very marge', the 'tanned harvesters', Endymion's 'shaping visions'

> Of colours, wings and bursts of spangly light

and Venus, with her fluttering scarf of blue

> over-spangled with a million
> Of little eyes,

which recalls the saffron wings, the honey drops, the blue rainbow of Iris—'rich scarf' to the 'proud earth'—all underlined by Keats.[1]

I do not suggest for a moment that there is any plagiarism or imitation on the part of Keats; on the contrary, we have here a very beautiful example of the creative stimulus and enrichment given

---

[1] This last passage

> The wind out-blows
> Her scarf into a fluttering pavillion;
> 'Tis blue, and over-spangled with a million
> Of little eyes, as though thou wert to shed,
> Over the darkest, lushest blue-bell bed,
> Handfuls of daisies.
> (*Endymion*, i. 627–32.)

is possibly a pretty example of one of those 'confluences of recollections' in a poet's brain, associations which fly together through the 'polarity of the imagination', of which Professor Lowes has recently given us so fascinating a study in his great book on Coleridge.

by the mature imagination of one great poet to the soaring and youthful imagination of another.

Keats's sensitiveness to imagery, phrases, sequence and groups of words, and rhythm in a poet he admired or encountered at an impressionable age has been made startlingly clear in Mr. Weller's recent careful study of the great influence upon him of the Irish poetess Mrs. Tighe, especially upon the *Eve of St. Agnes* and the great Odes.[1] That is a curious and most instructive example of the way in which poor, diluted, sentimental verse may form a part of the raw material for some of the most condensed and vigorous poetry in English.

It is almost needless to say that the influence of Shakespeare is of a different quality.

Verbal echoes there undoubtedly are:—of Ariel's song, in

> Who dives three fathoms where the waters run
> Gurgling in beds of coral,

of Prospero's 'cloud capp'd towers' in the 'palaces and towers of amethyst' seen by Peona, and her musings on

> the Morphean fount
> Of that fine element that visions, dreams,
> And fitful whims of sleep are made of,

Undoubtedly, as Miss Amy Lowell has pointed out (*Life of Keats*, i. 324), Keats is directly influenced here by his memory of Drayton's description in *Endimion and Phoebe* of Phoebe's

> Azur'd Mantle purfled with a vaile,
> Which in the Ayre puft like a swelling saile,
> Embosted Rayne-bowes did appeare in silk,
> With wauie streames as white as mornings Milk;

which he sees as a fluttering blue scarf embroidered in white, and goes on to illustrate this with the exquisite image of handfuls of daisies strewn on masses of dark bluebells. The 'embosted Rayne-bowes' are not reproduced, but it is worth noting that the passage in *The Tempest* which has certain affinities with both Drayton and Keats is the description of Iris,

> The queen o' the sky,
> Whose watery arch and messenger am I.

Was the rainbow, although forming no part of Keats's picture, possibly the link between the two passages in the poet's memory, which led him to combine recollections of them both in his own delicious and freshly imagined description?

[1] *Keats and Mary Tighe*, by Earle Vonard Weller, Publications of the Modern Language Association of America, Dec. 1927, pp. 963–85.

of his farewell to magic in Endymion's flight on the eagle,

> Down, down, uncertain to what pleasant doom,
> Swift as a fathoming plummet down he fell,

or of Caliban's seductive offers of rustic fare,

> Honey from out the gnarled hive I'll bring
> And apples, wan with sweetness, gather thee;[1]

reminiscences also, such as the description of the shipwreck so
curiously like the one with which *The Tempest* opens;[2] but the real
influence or rather kinship is of quite a different nature. It is almost
as if Keats, after living through the magical experiences and sights
and sounds of *The Tempest*, was still, when beginning his own poem,
so steeped in Shakespearian enchantment that the glamour of it is
carried over into the early adventures of his own hero, who actually
sees and hears similar sights and sounds and is stimulated by them
to visions of even greater and deeper beauty.

An exquisite example of what I mean is at the beginning of one
of the finest and most individual passages in the poem—character-
istically Keats—the description of the various sensations and
experiences which develop and complete humanity, rising from the
joys of the senses to the ecstasy of vision, through human love and
friendship to 'a love immortal'.

Endymion, answering the query, 'Wherein lies happiness?'
describes to Peona first the soothing touch of a roseleaf, then the
magic of sweet sound,

> hist, when the airy stress
> Of music's kiss impregnates the free winds
> And with a sympathetic touch unbinds
> Eolian magic from their lucid wombs.[3]

---

[1] I do not forget the passage in Ovid's *Metamorphoses* (Book XIII) where Polyphemus
offers similar joys to Galatea, a passage doubtless remembered by Shakespeare and Keats
alike, but it is only necessary to look at the parallel lines printed on pp. 58–9 below to see the
even more direct likeness to *The Tempest*.

[2] See below pp. 62–3; some parallel passages in *The Tempest, A Midsummer Night's
Dream*, and *Endymion*.

[3] This beautiful passage, Book I, lines 785–95, is trebly marked by Keats (with two
marginal lines and underlined) in his own copy of the first edition of *Endymion* now in the
Dilke Collection at Hampstead.

Could there be imagined a more perfect description than this of the essence of Ariel's being, spirit of ethereal music, 'free as mountain winds'?

From the next two lines we know that his songs are still ringing in the poet's ears,

> Old ditties sigh above their father's grave,

and so, launched, as it were, by echoes of the delicate music of Ariel, Keats rises to the magnificent and imperishable description of the ascent of the spirit of man by successive stages towards happiness.

This is the passage which he tells Taylor (30th Jan. 1818) was when he wrote it 'a regular stepping of the Imagination towards a truth'. Keats was right, as he generally was; it is a passage of inspired vision, but even he perhaps was unaware that the first impetus to it came from the 'sounds and sweet airs that give delight and hurt not' which he had listened to in Shakespeare's enchanted isle.

Sometimes it is an incident which has attracted and impressed him, and he sees it afresh, transmuting it to quite different uses, as when Endymion, wearied by his journey into the 'sparry hollows of the world', rests awhile,

> And thoughts of self came on, how crude and sore
> The journey homeward to habitual self!

and he illustrates the fitfulness and delusions of that journey with a reminiscence of the experiences of the 'men of sin' when Ariel by his tricks enticed them through 'tooth'd briars' into the 'filthy mantled pool':

> A mad-pursuing of the fog-born elf,
> Whose flitting lantern, through rude nettle briar,
> Cheats us into a swamp, into a fire,
> Into the bosom of a hated thing.[1]

---

[1] Here again I do not doubt that remembrances of Milton's 'wand'ring Fire' and of Puck are also present, but Ariel's mischievous pranks had been read and underlined, and the changes in the finished manuscript from nettle-*beds* to *briar*, from *bog* to *swamp*, and the addition of the last line, bring the whole very close to Ariel's adventure.

Or, again, a passage strikes him which either coincides with his own thought or possibly kindles it, as in the doubly marked lines of Ceres' blessing,

> Spring come to you at the farthest
> In the very end of harvest,

and one rather wonders why these so appeal to him, until one remembers the opening of *Endymion*, that poem begun

> Now while the early budders are just new,

with the wish that

> Autumn bold,
> With universal tinge of sober gold,
> Be all about me when I make an end.

It is scarcely surprising then that at the close, when Endymion returns to earth, he describes and takes leave of his experiences in terms which might equally well apply to the play which so rapturously delighted his creator just before he was brought to birth in a poet's brain;

> Caverns lone, farewell!
> And air of visions, and the monstrous swell
> Of visionary seas! No, never more
> Shall airy voices cheat me to the shore
> Of tangled wonder, breathless and aghast.

Keats was reading and eagerly marking *A Midsummer Night's Dream* at the same time as, or perhaps a little later than, *The Tempest*. Here again much in the atmosphere and setting is akin to his own poem. Both are steeped in moonlight and in the moon's influence; woods,

> Fresh breezes, bowery lawns and innocent floods,

form a common background; sweet-scented flowers, bees, butterflies, and glow-worms are the natural accompaniment to the woodland enchantment in each; but in spite of this the influence of Shakespeare's fairy tale on the early part of *Endymion* is not so all-pervading as is that of *The Tempest*.

PLATE 4

16   MIDSUMMER-NIGHT'S   ACT 2.

The ploughman lost his sweat; and the green corn
Hath rotted, ere his youth attain'd a beard:
The fold stands empty in the drowned field,
And crows are fatted with the murrain flock;
The nine men's morris is fill'd up with mud;
And the quaint mazes in the wanton green,
For lack of tread, are undistinguishable:
The human mortals want their winter here;
No night is now with hymn or carol blest:—
Therefore the moon, the governess of floods,
Pale in her anger, washes all the air,
That rheumatic diseases do abound:
And thorough this distemperature, we see
The seasons alter: hoary-headed frosts
Fall in the fresh lap of the crimson rose;
And on old Hyems' chin, and icy crown,
An odorous chaplet of sweet summer buds
Is, as in mockery, set: The spring, the summer,
The chiding autumn, angry winter, change
Their wonted liveries; and the 'mazed world,
By their increase, now knows not which is which:
And this same progeny of evils comes
From our debate, from our dissention;
We are their parents and original.

Obe. Do you amend it then; it lies in you:
Why should Titania cross her Oberon?
I do but beg a little changeling boy,
To be my henchman.

Tita.   Set your heart at rest.
The fairy land buys not the child of me.
His mother was a vot'ress of my order:
And, in the spiced Indian air, by night,
Full often hath she gossip'd by my side;
And sat with me on Neptune's yellow sands,
Marking the embarked traders on the flood;
When we have laugh'd to see the sails conceive,
And grow big-bellied, with the wanton wind;
Which she, with pretty and with swimming gait,
Would imitate; and sail upon the land,
(Following her womb, then rich with my young squire,)
To fetch me trifles, and return again,

SCENE 2.   DREAM.   17

As from a voyage, rich with merchandise,
But she, being mortal, of that boy did die;
And, for her sake, I do rear up her boy,
And, for her sake, I will not part with him.

Obe. How long within this wood intend you stay?

Tita. Perchance, till after Theseus' wedding-day.
If you will patiently dance in our round,
And see our moonlight revels, go with us;
If not, shun me, and I will spare your haunts.

Obe. Give me that boy, and I will go with thee.

Tita. Not for thy kingdom.—Fairies, away:
We shall chide down-right, if I longer stay.
[Exeunt Titania and her Train.

Obe. Well, go thy way: thou shalt not from this grove,
Till I torment thee for this injury.—
My gentle Puck, come hither: Thou remember'st
Since once I sat upon a promontory,
And heard a mermaid, on a dolphin's back,
Uttering such dulcet and harmonious breath,
That the rude sea grew civil at her song;
And certain stars shot madly from their spheres,
To hear the sea-maid's music.

Puck.   I remember.

Obe. That very time I saw, (but thou couldst not,)
Flying between the cold moon and the earth,
Cupid all arm'd: a certain aim he took
At a fair vestal, throned by the west;
And loos'd his love-shaft smartly from his bow,
As it should pierce a hundred thousand hearts:
But I might see young Cupid's fiery shaft
Quench'd in the chaste beams of the wat'ry moon;
And the imperial vot'ress passed on,
In maiden meditation, fancy-free.
Yet mark'd I where the bolt of Cupid fell:
It fell upon a little western flower,—
Before, milk-white; now purple with love's wound,—
And maidens call it, love-in-idleness.
Fetch me that flower; the herb I show'd thee once:
The juice of it on sleeping eyelids laid,
Will make or man or woman madly dote

A much read and thumbed page of *A Midsummer Night's Dream*

It takes the form rather of pictures that he remembers or of ideas
which have attracted him, which he re-embodies in his own poem.
A characteristic example of the way this works is to be seen in four
lines doubly marked by Keats (*M.N.D.* II. i. 159–62)[1]

> [Cupid all arm'd]
> . . . loos'd his love-shaft smartly from his bow,
> As it should pierce a hundred thousand hearts:
> But I might see young Cupid's fiery shaft
> Quench'd in the chaste beams of the wat'ry moon;

The idea of the moonbeam quenching the fiery dart of love pleases
him, and he reproduces it in the form of Endymion's prayer for
help:

> O Cynthia, ten times bright and fair!
> From thy blue throne, now filling all the air,
> Glance but one little beam of temper'd light
> Into my bosom, that the dreadful might
> And tyranny of love be somewhat scar'd!

Or he remembers the picture of Hermia and Helena embroidering
and singing together (*M.N.D.* III. ii. 203–8), and he sees it anew
in his description of Peona's arbour

> overwove
> By many a summer's silent fingering;
> To whose cool bosom she was us'd to bring
> Her playmates, with their needle broidery,
> And minstrel memories of times gone by.

This particular borrowing has been noticed by Miss Amy Lowell
(*Life of Keats*, i. 348–9), who points out that Severn had in May
1817 just completed his first oil painting, later (1819) exhibited at
the Royal Academy, which was a picture of this scene, suggested
to him by Keats, with this very quotation above it.[2]

---

[1] This passage is also underlined in the folio edition.

[2] *The Life and Letters of Joseph Severn*, by William Sharp, 1892, p. 45. It is worth
noting that in George Keats's letter to Severn, postmarked 22nd May, 1817 (*Life of
Severn*, pp. 17–18), a letter largely about this picture, he praises in the strongest terms
A Midsummer Night's Dream and *The Tempest*, saying he has read them both ' since

Miss Lowell would have been interested to know that Keats has doubly marked the passage in question (down the side as well as underlined) in his copy of Shakespeare.

Another reminiscence, this time of sweet sound, is of the music of Theseus's hounds and horn, also underlined (*M.N.D.* IV. i. 111–13, 115–16, 120–24, 126–31), and he seizes on the most beautiful and salient point in it, the reverberating echo from the mountain top, in Endymion's resolve:

> No, I will once more raise
> My voice upon the mountain-heights; once more
> Make my horn parley from their foreheads hoar:
> Again my trooping hounds their tongues shall loll
> Around the breathed boar.

So also the exquisite description of Endymion's eyelids, when they

> Widened a little, as when Zephyr bids
> A little breeze to creep between the fans
> Of careless butterflies:

contains an indirect but unmistakable recollection of Titania's order to her fairies to

> pluck the wings from painted butterflies,
> To fan the moon-beams from his sleeping eyes.

Undoubtedly, then, both these plays stirred and affected Keats profoundly at this time, and contribute quite definitely atmosphere and quality as well as words and phrases to the early part of *Endymion*, but the influence of *The Tempest* is the stronger of the two; it has kindled his imagination and stimulated his vision more continuously and profoundly, whereas the effect of the *Midsummer Night's Dream* is seen rather in isolated passages such as I have indicated.

So far we have noted in detail chiefly the markings of passages which specially delighted him either because they chimed with

I have been here', that is, at Hampstead, where he and Tom probably went the second week in April. Doubtless this was the result of John's enthusiasm at this time for these two plays, possibly before leaving London on the 14th of April.

ideas already surging in his brain, or because they stimulated him
to re-embody some part of them or started fresh visions of his
own.

Beyond these, in both plays, it is images and epithets which chiefly
enchant him.

One of the first lines he marks in *The Tempest* is Miranda's
description of her sensation on seeing the ship 'dashed all to
pieces',

> O, the cry did knock
> Against my very heart.

The intensity of feeling conveyed by this vivid physical image
clearly appeals to him, for all through the play he underlines it
wherever an echo of it recurs, as it does a little later in the same
scene,

> For still 'tis beating in my mind,

or in Prospero's advice to the King,

> Do not infest your mind with beating on
> The strangeness of this business

and his resolve after his great speech when the actors vanish,

> a turn or two I'll walk
> To still my beating mind.

which last five words in addition to underlining have two lines in
the margin.

We are not surprised, therefore, to find Isabella's counsel to
Angelo

> Go to your bosom;
> Knock there, and ask your heart what it doth know
> That's like my brother's fault,

similarly marked in *Measure for Measure*.

Naturally he underlines

> The fringed curtains of thine eye advance.

This metaphor, condemned—and misquoted—by Pope and

Arbuthnot,[1] and praised by Coleridge at length (Lect. IX, 1811–12), sank far into what Henry James would call 'the deep well' of Keats's 'unconscious cerebration', as did also that other in *Pericles*:

> Her eyelids, cases to those heavenly jewels
> Which Pericles hath lost, begin to part
> Their fringes of bright gold,

so that very early in *Endymion* we find a recollection of both fused together,

> Whose eyelids curtain'd up their jewels dim,

and a little later on a reminiscence of the first one alone,

> Those same full fringed lids a constant blind
> Over his sullen eyes.

Another passage in which Keats and Coleridge see eye to eye is where Prospero, telling Miranda of their enforced flight from Milan, says,

> i' the dead of darkness,
> The ministers for the purpose hurried thence
> Me and thy crying self.

Keats underlines the last two words, and would most surely have endorsed Coleridge's verdict on the power of the single word in poetry when he says, 'Here, by introducing a single happy epithet, "crying", in the last line, a complete picture is presented to the mind, and in the production of such pictures the power of genius consists' (Lect. IX, 1811–12).

We expect to find marked, as we do,

> In the dark backward and abysm of time

---

[1] In *The Art of Sinking in Poetry* as 'the Buskin, or *Stateley*', ... which 'raises what is base and low to a ridiculous visibility ... will not every true lover of the Profound be delighted to behold the most vulgar and low actions of life exalted in the following manner? ... See who is there?

> Advance the fringed curtains of thy eyes,
> And tell me who comes yonder.'

PLATE 5

TEMPEST. ACT 2.

Gon. And, do you mark me, sir?—

Alon. Pr'ythee, no more: thou dost talk nothing to me.

Gon. I do well believe your highness; and did it to minister occasion to these gentlemen, who are of such sensible and nimble lungs, that they always use to laugh at nothing.

Ant. 'Twas you we laugh'd at.

Gon. Who, in this kind of merry fooling, am nothing to you: so you may continue, and laugh at nothing still.

Ant. What a blow was there given!

Seb. An it had not fallen flat-long.

Gon. You are gentlemen of brave mettle: you would lift the moon out of her sphere, if she would continue in it five weeks without changing.

Enter ARIEL, *invisible, playing solemn Music.*

Seb. We would so, and then go a bat-fowling.

Ant. Nay, good my lord, be not angry.

Gon. No, I warrant you: I will not adventure my discretion so weakly. Will you laugh me asleep, for I am very heavy?

Ant. Go sleep, and hear us.

[*All sleep but Alon. Seb. and Ant.*

Alon. What, all so soon asleep! I wish mine eyes Would, with themselves, shut up my thoughts: I find, They are inclined to do so.

Seb. Please you, sir,

Do not omit the heavy offer of it:
It seldom visits sorrow; when it doth,
It is a comforter.

Ant. We two, my lord,
Will guard your person, while you take your rest,
And watch your safety.

Alon. Thank you: wondrous heavy.

[*Alonso sleeps. Exit Ariel.*

Seb. What a strange drowsiness possesses them!

Ant. It is the quality o'the climate.

Seb. Why
Doth it not then our eyelids sink? I find not
Myself dispos'd to sleep.

SCENE 1. TEMPEST. 27

Ant. Nor I; my spirits are nimble.
They fell together all, as by consent;
They dropp'd, as by a thunder-stroke. What might,
Worthy Sebastian?—O, what might?—No more:—
And yet, methinks, I see it in thy face,
What thou should'st be: the occasion speaks thee; and
My strong imagination sees a crown
Dropping upon thy head.

Seb. What, art thou waking?

Ant. Do you not hear me speak?

Seb. I do; and, surely,
It is a sleepy language; and thou speak'st
Out of thy sleep: what is it thou didst say?
This is a strange repose, to be asleep
With eyes wide open; standing, speaking, moving,
And yet so fast asleep.

Ant. Noble Sebastian,
Thou let'st thy fortune sleep—die rather; wink'st
Whiles thou art waking.

Seb. Thou dost snore distinctly;
There's meaning in thy snores.

Ant. I am more serious than my custom: you
Must be so too, if heed me; which to do,
Trebles thee o'er.

Seb. Well; I am standing water.

Ant. I'll teach you how to flow.

Seb. Do so: to ebb,
Hereditary sloth instructs me.

Ant. O,
If you but knew, how you the purpose cherish,
Whiles thus you mock it! how, in stripping it,
You more invest it! Ebbing men, indeed,
Most often do so near the bottom run,
By their own fear, or sloth.

Seb. Pr'ythee, say on:
The setting of thine eye, and cheek, proclaim
A matter from thee; and a birth, indeed,
Which throes thee much to yield.

Ant. Thus, sir:
Although this lord of weak remembrance, this

A page of *The Tempest*, with typical markings of lines and phrases

and
>   urchins
> Shall, for that vast of night that they may work,
> All exercise on thee,

both of which he quotes in his letter to Reynolds of the 17th of April 1817; but in addition to sheer beauty and imaginative quality he is continually attracted by quaintness and vividness of image, and

>   with age and envy
> Was grown into a hoop.

> to trash for over-topping
> They have chang'd eyes
> the heavy offer of it
> my strong imagination
> To the perpetual wink
> They'll take suggestion as a cat laps milk
> Dregs of the storm

are examples of the kind of phrase we find throughout underlined.

In the *Midsummer Night's Dream* it is above all the fairy poetry and songs he loves; he shows no sign of appreciation of the comic part. He marks or underlines nearly the whole of Act II, Sc. i[1] (Scenes i and ii in his edition, following Pope) up to l. 187, the speeches of Puck and the fairies, of Titania and Oberon, as also the opening fairy songs of Act II, Sc. ii (Sc. iii in his edition).

Otherwise, as in *The Tempest*, it is images,

> [the moon], like to a silver bow
> New bent in heaven,

> As wild geese that the creeping fowler eye,
> Or russet-pated choughs, many in sort,
> Rising and cawing at the gun's report
> Sever themselves, and madly sweep the sky;

---

[1] It is to the beginning of Titania's speech (II. i. 82) that he writes the long and interesting note in the folio edition, ending ' O Shakespeare, thy ways are but just searchable! The thing is a piece of profound verdure'; see p. 52 below.

pictures: such as Hermia and Helena lying 'upon faint primrose beds', the elves creeping into the acorn cups, Oberon's glorious sunrise over the sea; or vividness of phrase, such as

> the fierce vexation of a dream
> seething brains
> shaping fantasies
> wither'd dewlap
> toil'd their unbreathed memories
> tongue-tied simplicity

which he specially notes.

In the two other plays of which I have printed all the annotations (*Measure for Measure* and *Antony and Cleopatra*) there is no question of immediate influence on Keats's own work, as with *The Tempest* and in a lesser degree with *A Midsummer Night's Dream*. There is no need, therefore, for me to do more than draw attention to one or two points.

He marks doubly, both for matter and for manner as I take it (see p. 24 below), the Duke's great speech 'Be absolute for death' (III. i. 5–41); and, as always, he underlines throughout images and metaphors:—the three fine ones in the first scene, for instance, and the two vivid ones used by Claudio (I. ii. 135–9) on surfeit and fast and 'rats that ravin down their proper bane', or the succession of pictures in the Duke's description of the condition of Vienna (I. iii. 21–31), and so on.

He loves the quaint homely vigorous images:—

> And liberty plucks justice by the nose
>
> bite the law by the nose
>
> [thy head stands so tickle on thy shoulders] that a milk-maid, if she be in love, may sigh it off

and he notes vividness of phrase and epithet, especially of adjective:

> special soul
> most profound sciatica

fast my wife
drowsy and neglected act
heavy sense
my pith of business
devilish mercy
stinkingly depending
[Is it not] strange, and strange
paved bed

or little touches of dramatic imagination, such as the Provost's
question, 'What shall be done, sir, with *the groaning Juliet*?' which,
for the picture evoked by one word, might well go beside 'crying
self' already noted in *The Tempest*; or Pompey's remark to
Abhorson when he assured him that Barnadine

is coming, sir, he is coming, *I hear his straw rustle.*

He is interested in the movement of time in Act IV, Sc. i and ii;
the change from night to day, the irresistible march of the hours
towards Claudio's doom, and the way the tension of the watchers
is indicated, underlining each notation.

First Isabella announces she is to meet Angelo

Upon the heavy middle of the night,

then the Duke tells Mariana to make haste,

The vaporous night approaches.

The Provost showing Claudio the warrant for his death reminds
him

'Tis now dead midnight,

and later says no one has called 'since the curfew rang'.

As the hours go by and no reprieve comes, the Duke says,

As near the dawning . . . as it is,

the messenger, bringing the redoubled charge to execute Claudio
by four of the clock, remarks 'it is almost day'; and at the close
of the scene, when the Duke, after his long and anxious talk with
the Provost, without disclosing himself has gained four days respite

for Claudio and the tension is relieved, he glances upward out of the prison window and cries, '*Look, the unfolding star calls up the shepherd* ... Come away; *it is almost clear dawn*'.

The markings in *Antony and Cleopatra* are of the same type, and are applied chiefly to many of the great speeches, to images or vivid and remarkable expressions, such as,

> Scrupulous faction
> my salad days
> > Every time
> Serves for the matter that is then born in't.
>
> darting Parthia
> They are his shards, and he their beetle
> [Cleopatra] hath nodded him to her
> > Were it carbuncled
> Like holy Phoebus' car
> ... the Swan's down feather
> That stands upon the swell at full of tide,
> And neither way inclines.

Compare with this last

> Must not a woman be
> A feather on the sea,
> Sway'd to by every wind and tide?
> > (*Ode to Fanny*, early 1819?)

Antony and Cleopatra is one of the plays of which we can date with very close exactitude one at least of his readings, and almost certainly the reading during which he made these marks in his— then—new copy of Shakespeare.

Writing to Haydon from Margate on Sunday, May the 11th, 1817, in the letter which is full of Shakespeare and of Shakespeare quotations and echoes from start to finish, he says, 'It was very gratifying to meet your remarks on the manuscript'. This refers to a letter by Haydon contributed to the *Examiner* for May the 4th, 1817, on the subject of a book much under discussion at the time, *Manuscrit Venu de St. Hélène*. Keats goes on, 'I was reading Anthony and Cleopatra

when I got the Paper'. Allowing, therefore, two or three days for
the *Examiner* to reach Keats at Margate, he was reading and marking
this play between the 6th and 11th of May in the great Shakespearian
year 1817. Haydon himself links the topic to Shakespearian
psychology; he gives a series of acute reasons for his belief that this
life of Napoleon was dictated by himself and no other, and adds,
'all these and many more are touches of nature so true, of natural
self delusion so intense, and of Satanic defiance so deeply characteristic, as could only have come from the heart that gave birth to
them, or have been laid open by Shakespeare; and Shakespeare is
no longer alive'. Keats continues in his letter:

'There are several Passages applicable to the events you com-
mentate. You say that he [Napoleon] arrived by degrees and
not by any single struggle to the height of his ambition—and
that his Life had been as common in particulars as other Men's.
Shakespeare makes Enobarb say—

Where's Antony?

Eros.—He's walking in the garden, and *spurns*
    The rush that lies before him; cries, Fool, Lepidus!

In the same scene we find—

Let determined things
To destiny hold unbewailed their way.

Dolabella says of Anthony's Messenger,
    An argument that he is pluck'd when hither
    He sends so poor a pinion of his wing.

Then again—

Eno.—I see Men's Judgments are
    A parcel of their fortunes; and things outward
    Do draw the inward quality after them
    To suffer all alike.

The following applies well to Bertram [General Bertrand?]:

Yet he that can endure
To follow with allegiance a fallen Lord,
Does conquer him that did his Master conquer,
And earns a place i' the story.

But how differently does Buonaparte bear his fate from Anthony!'

All these quotations are underlined in Keats's Shakespeare, and the whole passage gives an interesting clue to the fact that Keats, like other readers, sometimes marked passages because they chimed with the thought in his mind at the moment or seemed applicable to it, as well as for their intrinsic or poetical worth.[1]

The two lines on spring and autumn in *The Tempest* (IV. i. 114–15), already noted, are another example of this, and one feels also that the Duke's words in *Measure for Measure* (V. i. 398–9)

> That life is better life, past fearing death,
> Than that which lives to fear

are marked as much because the man John Keats agreed passionately with the sentiment as for any particular beauty or quality in its expression noted by the poet.

I have examined very closely Keats's system of marking his books, and though it is not possible to say he has a definite system from which he never deviates, yet I believe the following holds good as a general rule.

When he considers a passage significant, either as throwing light on the character, or in the working out of the plot or for the thought it embodies, he often marks it down the side thus ⋮ or thus | and when, in addition, he admires an image or expression for its poetical and imaginative value, for vividness or beauty of phrase, he underlines it.

So we may find either one kind of marking or the other in a given passage; or quite often, both together.

An examination of the markings in *Antony and Cleopatra* illustrates very well what I mean.

The passage of dialogue between the lovers (I. iii. 13–29) revealing so much of Cleopatra's character and the way in which she manages Antony and plays upon him, including her attitude to Fulvia,

---

[1] Other instances of this are in *Troilus and Cressida* in the folio edition (see p. 46 below) or the note in *King Lear* (p. 43 below).

'the married woman', is marked down the side; but a little later on

> Eternity was in our lips and eyes

is underlined only.

The remarkable metaphor of the 'vagabond flag' (I. iv. 44–7) is underlined, but Caesar's speech describing Antony's character and temperament (I. iv. 55–71) is all marked down the side, and in addition seven lines which are remarkable for vividness of phrasing are under-scored.

Exactly the same system of marking is seen in Cleopatra's speech (I. v. 19–34) to Charmian, so revealing of her passionate preoccupation with Antony, of her imagination, and their mutual relationship, all marked down the side; but the great touches in it,

> demi Atlas of this earth
> the arm and burgonet of men
> serpent of old Nile
> Broad-fronted Caesar

are underlined as well.

The great final scene also (V. ii. 282–321) is all side-marked, but the underlined passages are:

> I am fire and air

> The stroke of death is as a lover's pinch
> Which hurts and is desired.

> ... spend that kiss,
> Which is my heaven to have,

and the final amazing imaginative touch of Charmian's farewell to her dead mistress whom she is about to follow,

> Your crown's awry;
> I'll mend it, and then play.

This explains why passages like the talk between the triumvirs (II. vii. 20–46), Cleopatra's immortal conversation with the messenger (III. iii. 7–48) or her final talk with her women (V. ii. 205–32) have side-marks only; why Cleopatra's astounding rush of simile and metaphor about Antony, 'His legs bestrid the ocean' (V. ii. 82–92), is underlined only, while the description of Cleopatra in her barge has both kinds of marking.

But the system is not invariably followed. Thus, what are perhaps the most exquisitely musical and poetically moving lines in the play, the great passage beginning

The crown o' the earth doth melt   (IV. xiii. 63–8)

are side-marked only, whereas Cleopatra's instructions to the messenger (II. v. 111–14), vividly interesting as a revelation of her character and attitude, but with no poetical value, are underlined.

On the whole, however, I think the principle represents Keats's method, and in other plays is well exemplified in the Duke's speech on death in *Measure for Measure* (III. i. 5–41) or in *A Midsummer Night's Dream*, II. i. 1–187 (in the Princeton copy, ii. 2, see Plate 4). It corresponds broadly too with the markings in the folio edition, and with those in George Keats's copy of the first canto of the *Faerie Queene*, which Miss Amy Lowell was sure were made by John Keats.[1]

It is noticeable that in *The Tempest* there are few passages with the double marking (underlining and dotted side-line); they are nearly all underlined only, as in Prospero's two great speeches (IV. i. 148–63 and V. i. 33–48), with the exception of the last line of the earlier speech

To still my beating mind,

which has two side-marks in addition.

This seems to show that he developed the dotted side-marking more fully later (for I am convinced *The Tempest* was the first to be marked) or else that the overpowering impression made upon him by this play was the poetical beauty and force of the individual lines and passages.

---

[1] Miss Lowell owned this book, and has printed the marked passages in her *Life of Keats*, vol. ii, App. C.

In the rare cases when the marks down the margin are two continuous lines, thus ‖, in addition to underlining, it indicates, I believe, very special admiration and appreciation of the whole passage, as in *The Tempest*, III. ii. 147–55; I. ii. 222–4, or *Measure for Measure*, IV. i. 41–3.

Other plays that are a good deal marked, though less than any of the four here printed, are *The Merchant of Venice*, *The Winter's Tale*, *Hamlet*, and *Macbeth*.

In the first of these the opening speeches of Antonio and Salarino are all marked down the side, and it is hardly necessary to say the opening of Act V (1–22) is similarly marked.

The passages I have noted as underlined are chiefly images, such as the picture of the 'scarfed bark', II. vi. 14–19, and

> Sit like his grandsire cut in alabaster.

> There are a sort of men whose visages
> Do cream and mantle like a standing pond

> The watery kingdom, whose ambitious head
> Spits in the face of heaven.

> A day in April never came so sweet
> To show how costly summer was at hand.

> How sweet the moonlight sleeps upon this bank.

> You may as well forbid the mountain pines
> To wag their high tops and to make no noise,
> When they are fretted with the gusts of heaven.

The marking of this last passage is interesting when one remembers Keats's own most wonderful image in the *Ode to Psyche* of the untrodden region of his mind

> Where branched thoughts, new grown with pleasant pain,
> Instead of pines shall murmur in the wind:
> Far, far around shall those dark-cluster'd trees
> Fledge the wild-ridged mountains steep by steep;

in which he takes the idea of the noise of the pines in the wind, possibly a reminiscence of this passage, and turns it to most subtle and imaginative uses in a way peculiarly his own.

In *The Winter's Tale* the merry-making pastoral (IV. iv; IV. iii in Keats's Shakespeare) is naturally a good deal underlined; for example, the great flower passage, and such touches as

> The marigold, that goes to bed wi' the sun
> And with him rises weeping.[1]
>
>   . . . the fann'd snow that's bolted
> By the northern blasts twice o'er.

In *Hamlet* also we find the markings we should expect, under the exquisite line

> The bird of dawning singeth all night long

and Horatio's description of the sunrise at the end of the first scene, Hamlet's 'O, that this too too solid flesh would melt' (I. ii), the speeches of Laertes and Ophelia in I. iii, and lines such as

> When I had seen this hot love on the wing,
> Would like the spring that turneth wood to stone
> Convert his gyves to graces.
>
> There lives within the very flame of love
> A kind of wick or snuff that will abate it.

Macbeth Keats read and marked a good deal; he ran his pen under some of the great passages, such as

> Canst thou not minister to a mind diseased   (V. iii. 40–5)
>
> To-morrow and to-morrow and to-morrow (V. v. 19–23)

as well as many images, for example

> The multiplying villanies of nature
> Do swarm upon him.
>
>   For the poor wren
> The most diminutive of birds will fight,
> Her young ones in her nest, against the owl.

---

[1] Probably as early as 1816, Keats knew and loved these lines, and remembered them in ll. 47–53 of 'I stood tip-toe upon a little hill'.

PLATE 6

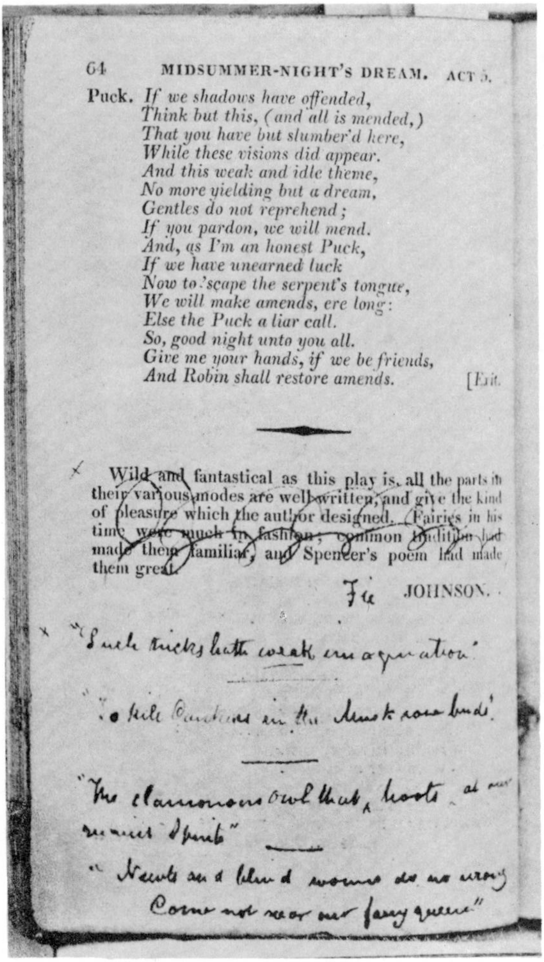

> 64   MIDSUMMER-NIGHT'S DREAM. ACT 5.
>
> *Puck. If we shadows have offended,*
> *Think but this, (and all is mended,)*
> *That you have but slumber'd here,*
> *While these visions did appear.*
> *And this weak and idle theme,*
> *No more yielding but a dream,*
> *Gentles do not reprehend;*
> *If you pardon, we will mend.*
> *And, as I'm an honest Puck,*
> *If we have unearned luck*
> *Now to 'scape the serpent's tongue,*
> *We will make amends, ere long:*
> *Else the Puck a liar call.*
> *So, good night unto you all.*
> *Give me your hands, if we be friends,*
> *And Robin shall restore amends.*   [*Exit.*
>
> Wild and fantastical as this play is, all the parts in
> their various modes are well written, and give the kind
> of pleasure which the author designed. Fairies in his
> time were much in fashion; common tradition had
> made them familiar, and Spencer's poem had made
> them great.
>
> JOHNSON.

Handwritten notes by Keats:

"Such tricks hath weak imagination"

"To kill Cankers in the Musk rose buds"

"The clamorous Owl that, hoots at our
quaint Spirits" ——

"Newts and blind worms do no wrong
Come not near our fairy queen"

Comments written by Keats on Johnson's
criticism

But float upon a wild and violent sea
Each way and move.

new sorrows
Strike heaven on the face.

my way of life
Is fall'n into the sear, the yellow leaf.

I have made notes of a good many other underlinings, but it seems to me that these, with the markings on the four plays printed in full, are sufficient to give a fairly comprehensive idea of Keats's method and of the type of passage which attracts his attention.

Another interesting fact which emerges from a study of these volumes is Keats's humorous impatience and scorn of Dr. Johnson's measured and matter of fact criticism of the plays. The edition has short general remarks selected from Johnson's criticism, and one or two from Steevens, printed at the end of every play (with the exception of *2 Henry VI*, *Pericles*, and *Cymbeline*), and Keats has expressed his views of these chiefly by quotations applied in a characteristic and unmistakable way.

At the end of *A Midsummer Night's Dream* (see Plate 6) when he has been revelling in poetry such as Oberon's

   . . . like a forester, the groves may tread,
Even till the eastern gate all fiery red
Opening on Neptune with fair blessed beams,
Turns into yellow gold his salt-green streams

and has just underlined

Every elf, and fairy sprite,
Hop as light as bird from brier;

it is somewhat of a cold douche to encounter at the close, printed almost as if it were a continuation to the play, Johnson's unimaginative dictum in his antithetical hammerlike rhythm:

'Wild and fantastical as this play is, all the parts in their various modes are well written, and give the kind of pleasure which the author designed. Fairies in his time were much in fashion; common tradition had made them familiar, and Spencer's poem had made them great.'

Keats scratches out the whole remark, slyly writes in 'Fie' before 'Johnson', and adds four quotations or adaptations from the play which appear to him apt:

> Such tricks hath *weak* imagination.
> To kill cankers in the Musk rose buds.
> The clamorous Owl that hoots at our quaint Spirits.
> Newts and blind worms do no wrong
> Come not near our faery queen,

and leaves it at that. As a commentary, it is comprehensive and crushing.

Johnson's real perception comes out in his remark on *Love's Labour's Lost* that, in spite of general censure, there is no play 'that has more evident marks of the hand of Shakespeare', but he balances this by saying earlier that 'there are many passages mean, childish, and vulgar; and some which ought not to have been exhibited, as we are told they were, to a maiden queen'. At the end of this Keats writes

> Who understandeth thee not loveth thee not.

After *The Winter's Tale* Johnson's patronizing remark beginning,

> This play, as Dr. Warburton justly observes, is, with all its absurdities, very entertaining,

is all scrabbled out, and at the end, under the great man's name is written 'lo fool again!' (see Plate 7).

The comment on *Measure for Measure* (see Plate 8) which is unusually long, and chiefly on the question of sources, has these lines firmly scored through:

> 'but the grave scenes, if a few passages be excepted, have more labour than elegance. The plot is rather intricate than artful. The time of the action is indefinite:'

PLATE 7

92   WINTER'S TALE.   ACT 5.

Thy father's court? for thou shalt hear, that I,—
Knowing by Paulina, that the oracle
Gave hope thou wast in being,—have preserv'd
Myself, to see the issue.
   Paul.   There's time enough for that;
Lest they desire, upon this push to trouble
Your joys with like relation.—Go together,
You precious winners all: your exultation
Partake to every one. I, an old turtle,
Will wing me to some wither'd bough; and there
My mate, that's never to be found again,
Lament till I am lost.
   Leon.   O peace, Paulina;
Thou should'st a husband take by my consent,
As I by thine, a wife: this is a match,
And made between's by vows. Thou hast found mine;
But how, is to be question'd: for I saw her,
As I thought, dead; and have, in vain, said many
A prayer upon her grave: I'll not seek far
(For him, I partly know his mind,) to find thee
An honourable husband:—Come, Camillo,
And take her by the hand: whose worth, and honesty,
Is richly noted; and here justified
By us, a pair of kings.—Let's from this place.—
What?—Look upon my brother:—both your pardons,
That e'er I put between your holy looks
My ill suspicion.—This your son-in-law,
And son unto the king, (whom heavens directing,)
Is troth-plight to your daughter.—Good Paulina,
Lead us from hence; where we may leisurely
Each one demand, and answer to his part
Perform'd in this wide gap of time, since first
We were dissever'd: Hastily lead away.   [*Exeunt.*

———

   This play, as Dr. Warburton justly observes, is, with
all its absurdities, very entertaining. The character of
Autolycus is naturally conceived, and strongly repre-
sented.   JOHNSON.

to fool again!

Keats's comment on Johnson's criticism
of *A Winter's Tale*

PLATE 8

82   MEASURE FOR MEASURE.

The novel of Giraldi Cinthio, from which Shakspeare is supposed to have borrowed this fable, may be read in *Shakspeare Illustrated*, elegantly translated, with remarks which will assist the inquirer to discover how much absurdity Shakspeare has admitted or avoided.

I cannot but suspect that some other had new-modelled the novel of Cinthio, or written a story which in some particulars resembled it, and that Cinthio was not the author whom Shakspeare immediately followed. The emperor in Cinthio is named Maximine: the duke, in Shakspeare's enumeration of the persons of the drama, is called Vincentio. This appears a very slight remark; but since the duke has no name in the play, nor is ever mentioned but by his title, why should he be called Vincentio among the *persons*, but because the name was copied from the story, and placed superfluously at the head of the list, by the mere habit of transcription? It is therefore likely that there was then a story of Vincentio duke of Vienna, different from that of Maximine emperor of the Romans.

Of this play, the light or comic part is very natural and pleasing, but the grave scenes, if a few passages be excepted, have more labour than elegance. The plot is rather intricate than artful. The time of the action is indefinite; some time, we know not how much, must have elapsed between the recess of the duke and the imprisonment of Claudio; for he must have learned the story of Mariana in his disguise, or he delegated his power to a man already known to be corrupted. The unities of action and place are sufficiently preserved.

JOHNSON.

Keats's comment on a portion of Johnson's criticism

and Keats writes underneath what has already been marked by
him in the play:

> But man! Proud man!
> Drest in a little brief authority
> Plays such fantastic tricks before high Heaven
> As makes the Angels weep.!!!

One wonders that he left out the line

> Most ignorant of what he's most assur'd.

That the remark on *As You Like It* has specially irritated Keats is
clear from the vigour and completeness with which it is crossed out
(see Plate 9). It is not so censorious as some of the other comments,
but the picture evoked of the Johnsonian dialogue between the
usurper and the hermit at the end of Shakespeare's witty and romantic comedy, and of the opportunity thus lost by the poet for giving
a moral lesson, is enough to warrant Keats's exasperated query, 'Is
Criticism a true thing?'[1]

He might well have added as an epitome of the fundamental
difference between himself and Shakespeare on the one hand and
Johnson on the other, the sentence in his letter to Woodhouse of
the 27th of Oct. 1818: 'What shocks the virtuous philosopher
delights the chameleon poet'.

The criticism on *Macbeth* (Plate 10) also calls forth Keats's
special ire, and it certainly sounds to modern ears extraordinarily
lacking in understanding: 'it has no nice discriminations of character; the events are too great to admit the influence of particular
dispositions, and the course of the action necessarily determines the
conduct of the agents'. Keats crosses and scratches the whole of
it out, appending caustically under Johnson's name,

> Thou losest Labour—
> As the Hare the Lion.

Keats's ingenuity in finding and adapting or piecing together,

---

[1] Touchstone's humorous complaint to Audrey (III. iii. 12), which it is now thought
contains a veiled reference to the manner of Marlowe's death, and which is very apt to Keats's
feeling, is written in on the same page by another hand, neither Keats's nor Severn's; it is the
only time it appears in the book. Keats has, however, underlined this passage in the text of
the play.

as here, suitable quotations from each play to express in Shakespeare's words his own feelings about Johnson is remarkable, and
very characteristic of his occasionally impish humour.

The Johnsonian remark at the end of *Antony and Cleopatra*,
which contains this sentence: 'the power of delighting is derived
principally from the frequent changes of the scene; for, except
the feminine arts, some of which are too low, which distinguish
Cleopatra, no character is very strongly discriminated', is
scratched out with peculiar vigour with lines in every direction,

thus    and below is written

> "Your Crown's awry;
> I'll mend it."

To the critical passage at the end of *All's Well*, which begins

'This play has many delightful scenes, though not sufficiently
probable; and some happy characters, though not new, nor
produced by any deep knowledge of human nature,'

and ends

'The story of Bertram and Diana had been told before of
Mariana and Angelo, and, to confess the truth, scarcely merited
to be heard a second time,'

Keats has merely appended, 'Wilt thou ever be a foul mouthed
calumnising (*sic*) knave?'

Indeed, the only passage of Johnson's criticism of which he shows
approbation is a sentence at the end of *The Two Gentlemen*:

'it will be found more credible, that Shakespeare might sometimes sink below his highest flights, than that any other should
rise up to his lowest.'

This is underlined.

Steevens meets with no more respectful treatment. There is a
remark of his, printed at the end of the *Comedy of Errors*, in which

PLATE 9

30   AS YOU LIKE IT.   ACT 5.

good epilogue, nor cannot insinuate with you in the
behalf of a good play? I am not furnished like a
beggar, therefore to beg will not become me: my way
is, to conjure you; and I'll begin with the women.
I charge you, O women, for the love you bear to men, to
like as much of this play as please them: and so I charge
you, O men, for the love you bear to women (as I
perceive by your simpering, none of you hate them),
that between you and the women, the play may please.
If I were a woman, I would kiss as many of you as
had beards that pleased me, complexions that liked me,
and breaths that I defied not: and, I am sure, as many
as have good beards, or good faces, or sweet breaths,
will, for my kind offer, when I make curt'sy, bid me
farewell.   [Exeunt.

Of this play the fable is wild and pleasing. I know
not how the ladies will approve the facility with which
both Rosalind and Celia give away their hearts. To
Celia much may be forgiven, for the heroism of her
friendship. The character of Jaques is natural and
well preserved. The comic dialogue is very sprightly,
with less mixture of low buffoonery than in some other
plays; and the graver part is elegant and harmonious.
By hastening to the end of this work, Shakspeare
suppressed the dialogue between the usurper and the
hermit, and lost an opportunity of exhibiting a moral
lesson, in which he might have found matter worthy of
his highest powers.

                         JOHNSON.

Is Criticism a true thing?

When a man's verses cannot
be understood, nor a man's

C. Whittingham, Printer, Chiswick.

wit seconded by the forward child,
understanding, it strikes a man more
dead than a great reckoning in

A vigorous method of dealing with
Johnsonian criticism

The quotation from As You Like It, III. iii. 12–15,
is not in Keats's script

PLATE 10

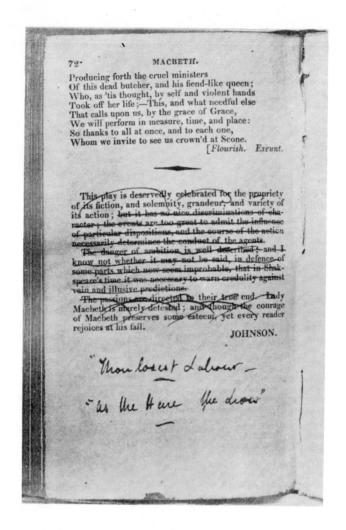

Keats's views on Johnson's criticism of
Macbeth
Notice the lines specially struck out

he says he does not hesitate to pronounce the play the composition
of two very unequal writers. Shakespeare undoubtedly had a share
in it, 'but that the entire play was no work of his, is an opinion
which (as Benedict says) "fire cannot melt out of me; I will die in
it at the stake"'. He compares the case of Plautus, who had plays
ascribed to him which were only retouched by him.

'In this comedy', he continues, 'we find more intricacy of plot
than distinction of character; and our attention is less forcibly
engaged, because we can guess in great measure how the dénoue-
ment will be brought about; yet the subject appears to have been
reluctantly dismissed, even in this last and unnecessary scene;
where the same mistakes are continued, till the power of affording
entertainment is entirely lost.'

This is signed 'Steevens', which Keats adorns thus:

'No Mr. Steevens
                    Sir
You are too wise, or
rather otherwise as the old phrase is.'

There are, throughout the volumes, only a very few textual notes
and emendations. The tiny pages do not offer much space for them,
and one can only regret that the margins had not been twice as
large, for the more roomy space in his folio edition did tempt
Keats to write some quite long notes, each one of which is unusual,
suggestive, and packed with thought.

The longest note in these little volumes is in the first scene of
Antony, when Cleopatra is at her most wayward on hearing of the
arrival of the messengers from Rome and Fulvia. Antony refuses
to hear them; Cleopatra urges that he should,

Fulvia perchance is angry.

This naturally strengthens his determination not to hear them,
and he turns to love and Cleopatra:

Let's not confound the time with conference harsh:
There's not a minute of our lives should stretch
Without some pleasure now. What sport to-night?

But again Cleopatra will only repeat,

Hear the ambassadors,

and Antony retorts,

Fie, wrangling queen!
Whom everything becomes, to chide, to laugh,
To weep; whose every passion fully strives
To make itself, in thee, fair and admired!

Keats puts a note to this last speech[1] (see Plate 11):

'How much more Shakespeare delights in dwelling upon the romantic and wildly natural than upon the monumental. See *Winter's Tale*, "When you do dance," etc.'

It is a charming and subtle point.

Keats is struck with the epithet 'wrangling', which at once and magically lowers the tone of the scene after Antony's magnificent burst of rhetoric:

Let Rome in Tiber melt,

and together with his loving and semi-jesting words that everything that she does becomes Cleopatra, brings the whole passage between the lovers down to the normal and natural.

He compares it to Florizel's similar assurance to Perdita in what is perhaps the most romantic and wildly natural scene in Shakespeare. Perdita has just distributed her flowers with words that have become immortal; she then, seeing the look of adoration in Florizel's eyes, is suddenly alarmed at her own forwardness, and says to him:

Come, take your flowers:
Methinks I play as I have seen them do
In Whitsun pastorals: sure this robe of mine
Does change my disposition.

And Florizel, like Antony, answers quickly and reassuringly:

What you do
Still betters what is done. When you speak, sweet,
I'ld have you do it ever: when you sing,

---

[1] Unfortunately the last few words have been cut off by the binder, but enough remains to make it out with the help of a glass.

PLATE 11

SCENE 2.   CLEOPATRA.   5

Cleo. Hear the ambassadors.
Ant.   Fie, wrangling queen!
Whom every thing becomes, to chide, to laugh,
To weep; whose every passion fully strives
To make itself, in thee, fair and admir'd!
No messenger; but thine and all alone,
To-night, we'll wander through the streets, and note
The qualities of people. Come, my queen;
Last night you did desire it :—Speak not to us.
                    [*Exeunt Ant. and Cleo. with their Train.*
Dem. Is Cæsar with Antonius priz'd so slight?
Phi. Sir, sometimes, when he is not Antony,
He comes too short of that great property
Which still should go with Antony.
Dem.   I'm full sorry,
That he approves the common liar, who
Thus speaks of him at Rome: But I will hope
Of better deeds to-morrow. Rest you happy!
                                    [*Exeunt.*

        SCENE 11.   *The same.   Another Room.*
Enter CHARMIAN, IRAS, ALEXAS, *and a Soothsayer.*
Char. Lord Alexas, sweet Alexas, most any thing
Alexas, almost most absolute Alexas, where's the sooth-
sayer that you praised so to the queen? O, that I knew
this husband, which, you say, must change his horns
with garlands!
Alex. Soothsayer.
Sooth. Your will?
Char. Is this the man?—Is't you, sir, that know things?
Sooth. In nature's infinite book of secresy,
A little I can read.
Alex.   Show him your hand.

            Enter ENOBARBUS.
Eno. Bring in the banquet quickly; wine enough,
Cleopatra's health to drink.
Char. Good sir, give me good fortune.
Sooth. I make not, but foresee.
Char. Pray then, foresee me one.
Sooth. You shall be yet far fairer than you are.

A note in *Antony and Cleopatra*

PLATE 12

TEMPEST. ACT 1.

Mira. Sir, most heedfully.
Pro. Being once perfected how to grant suits,
How to deny them; whom to advance, and whom
To trash for over-topping; new created
The creatures that were mine; I say, or chang'd them,
Or else new form'd them: having both the key
Of officer and officer, set all hearts
To what tune pleas'd his ear; that now he was
The ivy, which had hid my princely trunk,
And suck'd my verdure out on't.—Thou attend'st not:
I pray thee, mark me.
Mira. O good sir, I do.
Pro. I thus neglecting worldly ends, all dedicate
To closeness, and the bettering of my mind
With that, which, but by being so retir'd,
O'er-priz'd all popular rate, in my false brother,
Awak'd an evil nature: and my trust,
Like a good parent, did beget of him
A falsehood, in its contrary as great
As my trust was; which had, indeed, no limit,
A confidence sans bound. He being thus lorded,
Not only with what my revenue yielded,
But what my power might else exact,—like one,
Who having, unto truth, by telling of it,
Made such a sinner of his memory,
To credit his own lie,—he did believe
He was the duke; out of the substitution,
And executing the outward face of royalty,
With all prerogative:—Hence his ambition
Growing,—Dost hear?
Mira. Your tale, sir, would cure deafness.
Pro. To have no screen between this part he play'd,
And him he play'd it for, he needs will be
Absolute Milan: me, poor man!—my library
Was dukedom large enough; of temporal royalties
He thinks me now incapable: confederates
(So dry he was for sway) with the king of Naples,
To give him annual tribute, do him homage;
Subject his coronet to his crown, and bend
The dukedom, yet unbow'd (alas, poor Milan!)

SCENE 2. TEMPEST. 9

To most ignoble stooping. O the heavens!
Mira. O the heavens!
Pro. Mark his condition, and the event; then tell me,
If this might be a brother.
Mira. I should sin
To think but nobly of my grandmother:
Good wombs have borne bad sons.
Pro. Now the condition.
This king of Naples, being an enemy
To me inveterate, hearkens my brother's suit;
Which was, that he in lieu o'the premises,—
Of homage, and I know not how much tribute,—
Should presently extirpate me and mine
Out of the dukedom; and confer fair Milan,
With all the honours, on my brother: whereon,
A treacherous army levied, one midnight
Fated to the purpose, did Antonio open
The gates of Milan; and, i'the dead of darkness,
The ministers for the purpose hurried thence
Me, and thy crying self.
Mira. Alack, for pity!
I, not rememb'ring how I cried out then,
Will cry it o'er again; it is a hint,
That wrings mine eyes.
Pro. Hear a little further,
And then I'll bring thee to the present business
Which now's upon us; without the which, this story
Were most impertinent.
Mira. Wherefore did they not
That hour destroy us?
Pro. Well demanded, wench;
My tale provokes that question. Dear, they durst not;
(So dear the love my people bore me) nor set
A mark so bloody on the business; but
With colours fairer painted their foul ends.
In few, they hurried us aboard a bark;
Bore us some leagues to sea; where they prepar'd
A rotten carcase of a boat, not rigg'd,
Nor tackle, sail, nor mast; the very rats
Instinctively had quit it: there they hoist us,

A suggested emendation in *The Tempest*

I'ld have you buy and sell so, so give alms,
Pray so; and, for the ordering your affairs,
To sing them too: *when you do dance*, I wish you
A wave o' the sea, that you might ever do
Nothing but that; move still, still so,
And own no other function.

Keats here in a word or two puts his finger on a fundamental characteristic of Shakespeare, and one which has been startlingly emphasized by the production recently of *Hamlet* and *Macbeth* in modern dress. That is the essentially human naturalness of the presentation of even the most highly wrought and tragic of themes, as regards both the episodes and the dialogue.

This 'romantic and wildly natural' tone, as Keats calls it, is created, for example, in the midst of great tragedy, by the player and grave-digger scenes in *Hamlet* and the Lady Macduff and Porter scenes in *Macbeth*. The same effect is produced by the pastoral scenes in *The Winter's Tale*, following as they do upon the most tragic and highly wrought moments of Leontes' wrath and Hermione's dignified patience, and by the spoilt waywardness and feminine charm of Cleopatra in a play which has all the ingredients in setting, incident, and character for 'monumental' treatment.

In *The Tempest*, I. ii. 100, Keats suggests an emendation for a much debated line (see Plate 12). The folio reading is

> Like one
> Who hauing into truth, by telling of it,
> Made such a synner of his memorie
> To credite his owne lie,

clearly corrupt. In Keats's edition this is emended to

> Who having unto truth, by telling of it.

Keats suggests

> Who loving an untruth,

which has the advantage of making sense and of adding no extra syllables or letters; the 'l' for 'h' and the 'o' for 'a' would, from the handwriting point of view, be possible compositor's errors, although the 'un' for 'to' is less likely.

Hanmer (1744) had made the less good suggestion (needing more alteration)

> Who loving an untruth, and telling't oft
> Makes,

and Keats may have had an edition of his Shakespeare at hand and compared it. But for various reasons I incline to think this was not so, and that the note was his own idea jotted down in the course of his reading in order to make better sense of an obscure passage.

Mr. Dover Wilson's brilliant suggestion 'minted truth' is perhaps the more likely one because of the carrying on of the coinage metaphor later in the passage; still this note, if it is Keats's own, is enough to show us, did we need it, that if he had taken a hand with the great Shakespearian emendators the results would have been valuable.

One other emendation he makes in Oberon's speech (*Midsummer Night's Dream*, III. ii. 391, see Plate 13), which reads in Keats's copy:

> Even to the eastern gate, all fiery red,

Keats writes, 'Should it not be—till the eastern gate'.

The folio reading 'till' is clearly right, and Keats may, therefore, have been merely correcting it from his folio copy, although from its queried form I think this is not so. Like the note above, it is in pencil, and therefore was probably done at a different time from the other underlinings.

There are two little notes in *The Merry Wives*, of interest only because they illustrate with what close attention to details of characterization Keats read his Shakespeare.

In I. i. 113:

> '*Enter Sir John Falstaff, Bardolph, Nym and Pistol.*
>
> *Fal.* Now, Master Shallow; you'll complain of me to the King?'

Keats puts a cross against '*Fal.*' and notes, 'This is a way of

PLATE 13

Hel.   I will not trust you, I;
Nor longer stay in your curst company.
Your hands, than mine, are quicker for a fray;
My legs are longer though, to run away.   [*Exit.*
Her. I am amaz'd, and know not what to say.
                    [*Exit, pursuing Helena.*
Obe. This is thy negligence: still thou mistak'st,
Or else commit'st thy knaveries wilfully.
Puck. Believe me, king of shadows, I mistook.
Did not you tell me, I should know the man
By the Athenian garments he had on?
And so far blameless proves my enterprise,
That I have 'nointed an Athenian's eyes:
And so far am I glad it so did sort,
As this their jangling I esteem a sport.
Obe. Thou seest, these lovers seek a place to fight:
Hie therefore, Robin, overcast the night;
The starry welkin cover thou anon
With drooping fog, as black as Acheron:
And lead these testy rivals so astray,
As one come not within another's way.
Like to Lysander sometime frame thy tongue,
Then stir Demetrius up with bitter wrong;
And sometime rail thou like Demetrius:
And from each other look thou lead them thus,
Till o'er their brows death-counterfeiting sleep
With leaden legs and batty wings doth creep:
Then crush this herb into Lysander's eye;
Whose liquor hath this virtuous property,
To take from thence all error, with his might,
And make his eyeballs roll with wonted sight.
When they next wake, all this derision
Shall seem a dream, and fruitless vision;
And back to Athens shall the lovers wend,
With league, whose date till death shall never end.
Whiles I in this affair do thee employ,
I'll to my queen, and beg her Indian boy;
And then I will her charmed eye release
From monster's view, and all things shall be peace.
Puck. My fairy lord, this must be done with haste;
For night's swift dragons cut the clouds full fast,

And yonder shines Aurora's harbinger;
At whose approach, ghosts, wandering here and there,
Troop home to church-yards: damned spirits all,
That in cross-ways and floods have burial,
Already to their wormy beds are gone;
For fear lest day should look their shames upon,
They wilfully, themselves exile from light,
And must for aye consort with black-brow'd night.
Obe. But we are spirits of another sort:
I with the Morning's Love have oft made sport;
And, like a forester, the groves may tread,
Even to the eastern gate, all fiery red,
Opening on Neptune with fair blessed beams,
Turns into yellow gold his salt-green streams.
But, notwithstanding, haste; make no delay:
We may effect this business yet ere day. [*Exit Oberon.*
Puck. Up and down, up and down,
    I will lead them up and down:
    I am fear'd in field and town:
    Goblin, lead them up and down.
Here comes one.

        Enter LYSANDER.

Lys. Where art thou, proud Demetrius? speak thou
    now.   [thou?
Puck. Here villain; drawn and ready. Where art
Lys. I will be with thee straight.   Follow me then
Puck.   [thou?
To plainer ground. [*Exit Lys. as following the Voice.*

        Enter DEMETRIUS.

Dem.   Lysander! speak again.
Thou runaway, thou coward, art thou fled?
Speak. In some bush? Where dost thou hide thy
    head?
Puck. Thou coward, art thou bragging to the stars,
Telling the bushes that thou look'st for wars,
And wilt not come? Come, recreant; come, thou child;
I'll whip thee with a rod: He is defil'd
That draws a swoid on thee.

An emendation in *A Midsummer Night's Dream*

PLATE 14

50   TITUS ANDRONICUS.   ACT 2.

Sat. If it be prov'd! you see, it is apparent.—
Who found this letter? Tamora, was it you?
Tam. Andronicus himself did take it up.
Tit. I did, my lord: yet let me be their bail:
For by my father's reverend tomb, I vow,
They shall be ready at your highness' will,
To answer their suspicion with their lives.
Sat. Thou shalt not bail them: see, thou follow me.
Some bring the murder'd body, some the murderers:
Let them not speak a word, the guilt is plain;
For, by my soul, were there worse end than death,
That end upon them should be executed.
Tam. Andronicus, I will entreat the king;
Fear not thy sons, they shall do well enough.
Tit. Come, Lucius, come; stay not to talk with them.
                          [*Exeunt severally.*

SCENE V. *The same.*

Enter DEMETRIUS *and* CHIRON, *with* LAVINIA, *ravished; her Hands cut off, and her Tongue cut out.*

Dem. So, now go tell, an if thy tongue can speak,
Who 'twas that cut thy tongue, and ravish'd thee.
Chi. Write down thy mind, bewray thy meaning so;
And, if thy stumps will let thee, play the scribe.
Dem. See, how with signs and tokens she can scowl.
Chi. Go home, call for sweet water, wash thy hands.
Dem. She hath no tongue to call, nor hands to wash;
And so let's leave her to her silent walks.
Chi. An 'twere my case, I should go hang myself.
Dem. If thou hadst hands to help thee knit the cord.
                          [*Exeunt Demetrius and Chiron.*

Enter MARCUS.

Mar. Who's this,—my niece, that flies away so fast?
Cousin, a word; Where is your husband!—
If I do dream, 'would all my wealth would wake me!
If I do wake, some planet strike me down,
That I may slumber in eternal sleep!—
Speak, gentle niece, what stern ungentle hands
Have lopp'd, and hew'd, and made thy body bare

Keats's views on a portion of *Titus
Andronicus*

Falstaff's, vid. "Hen. 4th." Mast^r. Shallow I owe you a thousand pounds'.

A little later, in III. v. 61,

> ' *Enter Ford.*
>
> *Ford.* Bless you sir!
>
> *Fal.* Now, Master Brook; you come to know what hath passed between me and Ford's wife?'

Keats again puts a cross against '*Fal.*' and notes, 'Another instance of Falstaff's peculiar way'.

In *Titus Andronicus* Keats has by a very swift and simple method left his contribution to the vexed question of Shakespeare's authorship. He has scratched out with his pen the whole of Act II, Sc. iii, 259–306, and Sc. iv. 1–15—the episode where Tamora produces the letter throwing on the two sons of Andronicus the guilt of the murder of Bassianus, whom she has just seen murdered by her own two sons, and the horrible passage which follows in which Demetrius and Chiron jeer at the mutilated Lavinia (see Plate 14). He has also struck out at the end V. iii. 156–71, 182–204 (see Plate 15).

No one, I imagine, has ever thought the earlier passage was by Shakespeare, but it is worth noting that the beginning of Lucius's speech,

> Come hither, boy; come, come, and learn of us
> To melt in showers: (V. iii. 160–8)

is one of the few passages which has something of a Shakespearian ring. Keats, however, has deliberately struck it out.

Through the play he has underlined four lines only:

II. i. 7, 8.   Gallops the zodiac in his glistering coach,
           And overlooks the highest-peering hills:

II. iii. 230. And shows the ragged entrails of the pit:

and the first of the two lines of the whole play which cry Shakespeare as author,

II. ii. 1.   The hunt is up, the morn is bright and grey.

But although he marks little, and deliberately deletes some, yet he
sees Shakespeare's hand in it, for he clearly strongly disagrees with
Johnson's wholesale judgement of the play as spurious (see Plate 15),
and has written in at the foot this quotation from *Julius Caesar*:

> Ye Blocks, ye stones! Ye worse than senseless things
> Knew ye not Pompey?

Keats's volume of Shakespeare's *Poems*, which is now in the
Hampstead Public Library, belonged to his friend John Hamilton
Reynolds, who gave it to Keats in 1819, as is inscribed in Reynolds's
writing on the title-page.

Reynolds was, of all his friends, the one who had most real
understanding of the poet in Keats; he was, as regards poetry, his
most sympathetic correspondent, and so it is in the letters to him
that we find some of the most subtle and valuable literary criticism
and reflection. Keats's friends were in the habit of lending each
other books, and it is possible that Reynolds lent this volume to
Keats some time before he actually gave it him for his own. At any
rate the first reference we have to a reading of the Sonnets is in the
letter he wrote to Reynolds a day or two after his arrival at Burford
Bridge on the 22nd of November 1817, in which he says:

> 'One of the three books I have with me is Shakespeare's Poems:
> I never found so many beauties in the Sonnets—they seem to
> be full of fine things said unintentionally—in the intensity of
> working out conceits. Is this to be borne? Hark ye!

> > When lofty trees I see barren of leaves,
> > Which erst from heat did canopy the head [*sic*]
> > And Summer's green all girded up in sheaves
> > Borne on the bier with white and bristly head.' [*sic*]

This sonnet (XII) is marked all down the side in the volume of
the *Poems*, with a little extra zigzag mark opposite the last two lines
quoted above.

Keats continues:

> 'He has left nothing to say about nothing or anything:
> for look at snails—you know what he says about Snails—

PLATE 15

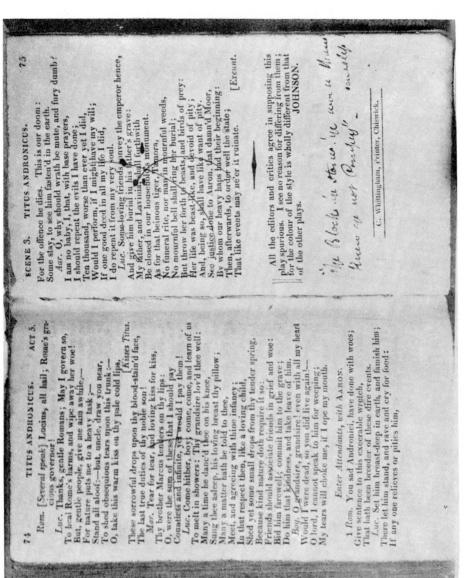

Keats's contribution to the question of the Shakespearian authorship of *Titus*

you know when he talks about " cockled Snails "—well, in one
of these sonnets, he says—the chap slips into—no! I lie! this is
in the "Venus and Adonis": the simile brought it to my Mind.

> As the snail, whose tender horns being hit,
>   Shrinks back into his shelly cave with pain,
> And there all smothered up in shade doth sit,
>   Long after fearing to put forth again;
> So at his bloody view her eyes are fled,
> Into the deep dark Cabins of her head.[1]

He overwhelms a genuine Lover of poesy with all manner of
abuse, talking about—

> "a poet's rage
> And stretched metre of an antique song."

Which, by the bye, will be a capital motto for my poem, won't it?

He speaks too of "Time's antique pen"—and "April's first-
born flowers"—and "Death's eternal cold".'

In the volume of *Poems* all these are underlined, as well as marked
with two side-lines.

We cannot be grateful enough to Reynolds for calling forth this
glimpse of what the sonnets meant to Keats, and of how greatly
their exquisite verbal music excited him. But even if we had not
this letter, we need only turn over a few pages in his marked
copy to see with what passionate interest and excitement he read
them. They are marked all through in ink. Some few of these
marks, and, I believe, all the notes, of which there are very few, are
by Reynolds. There are some pencil markings by Woodhouse; for
instance the line 'My name be buried where my body is' in sonnet
LXXII, has a pencil cross beside it, and 'Keats' in Woodhouse's script
is written against it. But by far the greatest amount of marking is by
Keats, who has very specially picked out the following sonnets, that
is, he has scored them all down one side and has in addition marked
again certain lines in them, the numbers of which are given in brackets:

---

[1] The misquotations in the second and fourth lines of this passage have always puzzled
me. Those in the sonnet are, I imagine, a slip in writing, but that a poet with Keats's
sensitiveness for words should have written 'back into' for 'backward in' and '*put* forth'
for '*creep* forth' is not what one would expect.

II (7, 12, 14), V (5, 6, 10), VII (8, 10), VIII (10), XII (7, 8), XIII (11, 12), XV, XVI (5), XVII (9, 12), XVIII (two marks down the side, lines 9, 12, and 14 underlined each with two extra side-marks, and lines 2 and 3 with extra side-marks, see Plate 16), XIX (4, 10, 14), XX, XXI (7, 8, 11, 12), XXII, XXIII (14), XXV (6, 7, 9), XXVII (1, 2, 5, 6, 7, 8, two side-lines all the way, and three extra opposite ll. 5–8 as well as underlining), XXVIII, XXIX (9–14), XXXII (1, 5, 10–14), XXXIII (3, 4, 7), XXXIV (13, 14), LII (4, 8), LIII (1, 2), LX (10, 11, three side-lines all down), LXVI (13, 14), LXXIII (3), LXXVI (6), LXXXIII, LXXXVI (1–4, 9, 10), LXXXVII (1), XCIII (9), XCV (7), XCVII (not all marked, but ll. 4, 6–8 underlined and 9–14 marked at side), XCVIII (14 doubly underlined), CVI (three side-lines all down and ll. 3–5 very specially marked), CX (1–4), CXI, CXVI (four side-lines, ll. 12 and 14 underlined), CXXIII (5, 6), CXXVIII (4, 6, 11), CXXX, CXLVI.

In addition, many single lines and phrases are specially marked, such as:

How many a holy and obsequious tear
Hath dear religious love stol'n from mine eye

Where summer's breath their masked buds discloses

When I have seen the hungry Ocean gain
Advantage on the Kingdom of the shore

O, how shall summer's honey breath hold out

Come in the rearward of a conquer'd woe

And buds of majoram had stol'n thy hair

As *Philomel* in summer's front doth sing

Three April perfumes in three hot Junes burn'd

And truly not the morning Sun of Heaven
Better becomes the grey cheeks of the East

sweet silent thought

thy straying youth

soundless deep

my Adder's sense

million'd accidents

PLATE 16

130 *SONNETS.*

XVIII.

Shall I compare thee to a fummer's day ?
Thou art more lovely and more temperate :
Rough winds do fhake the darling buds of May,
And fummer's leafe hath all too fhort a date :
Sometime too hot the eye of heaven fhines,
And often is his gold complexion dimm'd ;
And every fair from fair fometime declines,
By chance, or nature's changing courfe, untrimm'd ;
But thy eternal fummer fhall not fade,
Nor lofe poffeffion of that fair thou oweft ;
Nor fhall death brag thou wander'ft in his fhade,
When in eternal lines to time thou groweft :
  So long as men can breathe, or eyes can fee,
  So long lives this, and this gives life to thee.

XIX.

Devouring Time, blunt thou the lion's paws,
And made the earth devour her own fweet brood ;
Pluck the keen teeth from the fierce tyger's jaws,
And burn the long-liv'd phœnix in her blood ;
Make glad and forry feafons as thou fleet'ft,
And do whate'er thou wilt, fwift-footed Time,
To the wide world, and all her fading fweets ;
But I forbid thee one moft heinous crime :
O carve not with thy hours my love's fair brow,
Nor draw no lines there with thine antique pen ;
Him in thy courfe untainted do allow,
For beauty's pattern to fucceeding men.
  Yet, do thy worft, old Time : defpite thy wrong,
  My love fhall in my verfe ever live young.

A page from Keats's copy of Shakespeare's *Poems*, now in the
Hampstead Library, showing his method of marking the Sonnets

One cannot but think some of the markings here, as in *Troilus and Cressida*, were made during the years 1819 and 1820, when he was suffering from love's burning fever.   Such are :

> ＊ O how can Love's eye be true,
>   That is so vex'd with watching and with tears?

underlined with double side-marks;

>   Tired with all these, from these would I be gone,
>   Save that to die, I leave my love alone,

with four side-marks and the last line underlined;

>   So are you to my thoughts as food to life,
>   Or as sweet-season'd showers are to the ground,

doubly marked;

>   Is it thy will thy image should keep open
>   my heavy eyelids to the weary night?

trebly marked, and the similar thought in XXVII, 5–8, with six marks; or the last six lines of XCII, the last three with trebled side-lines, and the first eleven lines of CXXXVIII.

Lucrece is not much marked; *Venus and Adonis* has a few marks, chiefly stanzas 15* , 24 (1, 2, 5, 6), 25* (4), 26 (2, 3), 32* (3), 50*, 59,* 61* (2, 3), 76*, 81* (2), 82 (3–6), 88 (2), 91*, 136 (5, 6), 142 (3, 4), 143 (1–4), 154* (2), 163 (2), 172 (1, 2), 173 (1–4), 182*. Those with an asterisk have the entire stanza marked down the side, and the numbers in brackets refer to lines specially marked.

Some of these lines made a very deep impression, and we catch a definite echo of at least three of them:

>   My smooth moist hand, were it with thy hand felt,
>   Would in thy palm dissolve, or seem to melt. (24, ll. 5, 6)
>   Her other tender hand his fair cheek feels :   (59, l. 4)

in the query of Lycius to Lamia

>   Why do you shudder, love, so ruefully?
>   Why does your tender palm dissolve in dew?

A Lover's Complaint has been much read and has a good deal of marking, some of it almost certainly by Reynolds, and it is on the blank leaf facing the heading of this poem that Keats wrote out, on board ship, on the evening of his last day spent on English soil, what are, so far as we know, the latest lines of his own poetry his hand penned. This is the famous sonnet (see Plate 17), composed in the early days of his engagement to Fanny Brawne (Feb. 1819), the opening line of which is the summing up, I believe, in his own mind, of his final aspiration and attitude to the spirit of Shakespeare:

Bright star, would I were stedfast as thou art.

Keats's copy of the 1808 reprint of the Shakespeare folio of 1623 is a precious volume belonging to the Dilke Collection, and it is now kept at the Keats House at Hampstead. He got it, as he did the small edition, in 1817, which date is written in after his name on the title-page.

Only five plays in it are marked. Of these the most underlined is *Troilus and Cressida*, which has in addition five notes out of a total of nine in the volume; so it was in the folio edition that he read and studied this play with minute attention and appreciation. *King Lear* is underlined throughout, with three notes; a large part of *A Midsummer Night's Dream*, II. i. 82–164, is underlined and has one note; and there is a little marking in the early parts of *Romeo and Juliet* and of *Henry IV*, Part I.

The first (indirect) reference we have to this volume is early in 1818, when Keats writes to Bailey from Hampstead (23rd Jan.) and puts in his letter the Lines on seeing a Lock of Milton's Hair. He tells him he had sat down the previous day to read *King Lear*, 'and felt the greatness of the thing up to the Writing of a Sonnet preparatory thereto'. In a letter of the same date to his brothers, who were then at Teignmouth, he transcribes the now famous sonnet 'On sitting down to read King Lear once again'. Both these poems are written out in Keats's hand in his folio edition, and he probably wrote them on the 22nd of January 1818.

We next hear of this book during those depressingly wet weeks later on in the spring when George came up to town to prepare for

Bright Star, would I were stedfast as thou art—
Not in lone splendor hung aloft the night
And watching, with eternal lids apart,
Like nature's patient sleepless Eremite,
The moving waters at their priestlike task
Of pure ablution round earth's human shores,
Or gazing on the new soft-fallen masque
Of snow upon the mountains and the moors.
No—yet still stedfast, still unchangeable.
Pillow'd upon my fair love's ripening breast,
To feel for ever its soft swell and fall,
Awake for ever in a sweet unrest,
Still, still to hear her tender-taken breath,
And so live ever—or else swoon to death.

Charles Brown writes, sending a letter from Severn
from Rome, Sept 19th 1821, published by me in
Athenæum 23 aug 1879, "He wrote this sonnet in
the ship — it is one of his most beautiful things. I will
send it." This was I think Keats' last poem, &
it ends with the word Death.

Sonnet written by Keats on a blank leaf facing the heading of
A Lover's Complaint in his copy of Shakespeare's *Poems*
*The note below is written by Sir Charles Dilke, who bought the book at
Sotheran's sale in April* 1881

PLATE 18

||Horfe buttered his Hay.

Enter Cornewall, Regan, Gloster, Seruants.

Lear. Good morrow to you both.
Corn. Haile to your Grace. *Kent here set at liberty.*
Reg. I am glad to fee your Highneffe.
Lear. Regan, I thinke your are . I know what reafon
I haue to thinke fo, if thou fhould'ft not be glad,
I would diuorce me from thy Mother Tombe,
Sepulchring an Adultreffe. O are you free?
Some other time for that. Beloued *Regan,*
Thy Sifters naught: oh *Regan,* fhe hath tied
Sharpe-tooth'd vnkindneffe, like a vulture heere,
I can fcarce fpeake to thee, thou'lt not beleeue
With how deprau'd a quality. Oh *Regan.*
Reg. I pray you Sir, take patience, I haue hope
You leffe know how to value her defert,
Then fhe to fcant her dutie.
Lear. Say? How is that?
Reg. I cannot thinke my Sifter in the leaft
Would faile her Obligation. If Sir perchance
She haue refrained the Riots of your Followres,
'Tis on fuch ground, and to fuch wholefome end,
As cleeres her from all blame.
Lear. My curfes on her.

Lear. Who put my man i'th'Stockes?
Enter Steward.
Corn. What Trumpet's that?
Reg. I know't, my Sifters: this approues her Letter,
That fhe would foone be heere. Is your Lady come?
Lear. This is a Slaue, whofe eafie borrowed pride
Dwels in the fickly grace of her he followes.
Out Varlet, from my fight.
Corn. What meanes your Grace?
Enter Gonerill.
Lear. Who ftockt my Seruant? *Regan,* I haue good hope
Thou did'ft not know on't.
Who comes here? O Heauens!
If you do loue old men; if your fweet fway
Allow Obedience; if you your felues are old,
Make it your caufe: Send downe, and take my part.
Art not afham'd to looke vpon this Beard?
O *Regan,* will you take her by the hand?
Gon. Why not by'th'hand Sir? How haue I offended?
All's not offence that indifcretion findes,
And dotage termes fo.
Lear. O fides, you are too tough!
Will you yet hold?
How came my man i'th'Stockes?
Corn. I fet him there, Sir: but his owne Diforders
Deferu'd

Part of a page of *King Lear* (II. iv) in Keats's folio Shakespeare

One leaf only in the folio intervenes between this passage and the later one where the words 'poore Tom' are underlined and dated. The tiny sketch of mountains on the right here is almost surely a reminiscence of his Scotch tour (compare the little drawing in his letter to Tom of July 17, 1818), and would indicate that it, and probably the underlining, were done during the same reading, while he sat by Tom's bedside on Sunday evening, October 4, 1818

his departure to America, and John joined the invalid Tom in the 'splashy, rainy, misty, snowy, foggy, haily, floody, muddy, slipshod county' of Devonshire.

He writes to Reynolds (27th April) that he has sent for his folio Shakespeare, 'in which there are the first few stanzas of my "Pot of Basil"'. He had finished *Isabella*, and wished to transcribe the whole, and these early stanzas must have been on loose sheets slipped into the Shakespeare, for there is nothing of the kind there now.

By the end of June he was off to Scotland with Brown, returning at the end of August to find Tom very ill; and until the 1st of December, when he died, Keats was in close attendance upon him. On the 21st of September he writes to Dilke, 'I wish I could say Tom was any better. His identity presses upon me so all day that I am obliged to go out . . . to write and plunge into abstract images to ease myself of his countenance, his voice, and feebleness.'

We know that he tried 'plunging' into Shakespeare to ease his mind, for in his folio edition there is a pathetic note in *King Lear*, III. iv, where the words 'poore Tom' are underlined, and the date, 'Sunday evening, Oct. 4, 1818' written beside them. Later in this month he was, almost certainly, still reading in his folio, this time *Troilus and Cressida*, for towards the end of the long journal letter finished on his birthday, the 31st of October, and sent to George and Georgiana in America, he says:

'I feel more and more every day, as my imagination strengthens, that I do not live in this world alone but in a thousand worlds. No sooner am I alone than shapes of epic greatness are stationed around me, and serve my Spirit the office which is equivalent to a King's body-guard. . . . According to my state of mind I am with Achilles shouting in the Trenches, or with Theocritus in the Vales of Sicily. Or I throw my whole being into Troilus, and repeating those lines, 'I wander like a lost Soul upon the Stygian Banks staying for waftage', I melt into the air with a voluptuousness so delicate that I am content to be alone.'

It is in his next long letter to his brother and sister in America (Dec. 1818–Jan. 1819), after Tom's death, when he clearly is poignantly conscious of the vast distance which separates them, that he suggests they each shall read a passage of Shakespeare every Sunday at ten o'clock, 'and we shall be as near each other as blind bodies can be in the same room'.

In the meantime, probably in October 1818, Keats had met and fallen in love with Fanny Brawne. His first careless but self-conscious mention of her is in this same letter, and from this time to the end his love for and interest in Shakespeare are deepened and heightened by a consciousness that they endured the agony of a similar experience—a passionate, all-devouring, frustrated, and devastating love, against the thraldom of which one part of their natures struggled and rebelled. From now on Shakespeare, in addition to being a supreme artist, the source of witching music, magical phrase and image, is also the 'miserable and mighty Poet of the human Heart',[1] a fellow sufferer who has felt what Keats is feeling, who has come through pain comparable to Keats's own, and has emerged serene and poised. 'The middle age of Shakespeare', he writes, 'was all clouded over; his days were not more happy than Hamlet's who is perhaps more like Shakespeare himself in his common every day Life than any other of his characters.'[2]

Of his effort later in that summer of 1819 to carry on his work by steeling his heart ('my heart seems now made of iron', 16th Aug. 1819) against all he loved best, by shutting out Fanny Brawne and the whole world of men and women, by substituting Milton for Shakespeare, in short by denying his own real nature, we can read in his letters, the evidence in which Mr. Murry has interpreted and developed into a moving and convincing narrative.[3] The return, after bitter anguish and struggle, to his natural self is expressed in the great Ode to Autumn, the most poised and mellow poem, the most Shakespearian in mood and feeling that Keats ever wrote.

So it is that from the time of those soft and sunny September days in Winchester to the end, Shakespeare is nearer to him than ever; not only as ideal poet but also as close intimate human friend

---

[1] Letter to Miss Jeffrey, 9th June 1819. [2] *Ibid.*
[3] *Keats and Shakespeare*, chap. xi.

and companion, who would have understood him as no one else could; who would have understood even those passionate, desperate, sweet, bitter, ecstatic and agonized letters to the woman he loved. 'What would Rousseau have said at seeing our . . . correspondence', he asks her in February 1820, 'I don't care much—I would sooner have Shakespeare's opinion about the matter.'

And six months later, when writing that terrible letter, probably the last he sent her, which shows his pain at the thought of parting with her as he knows for ever and his even greater pain at seeing her at intervals and then leaving her—'I cannot bear flashes of light and return into my glooms again'—and which lays bare his torturing, jealous uncertainty of her and revulsion of feeling—in this moment of the supreme anguish of his spirit, once more it is to Shakespeare he turns—

'Shakespeare always sums up matters in the most sovereign manner. Hamlet's heart was full of such Misery as mine is when he said to Ophelia "Go to a Nunnery, go, go!" Indeed I should like to give up the matter at once—I should like to die. I am sickened at the brute world which you are smiling with. I hate men, and women more.'

This is the mood of *Troilus and Cressida*, the mood of the sensitive, imaginative, idealistic poet in bitter anguish, revolting in bewilderment and disgust from the pain, the lack of comprehension, the brutality of the world. There is no doubt that he was reading and re-reading the play at this time (the spring and summer of 1820), and seeing re-enacted in himself the anguish of the betrayed Troilus. 'My greatest torment since I have known you', he writes to Fanny a few days after his seizure on the 3rd of February 1820, 'has been the fear of you being a little inclined to the Cresseid.' The knowledge that she does not love him as he does her, a mistrust of the capacity, depth, and loyalty of her nature, this, if physical disease was killing his body, was the more insidious disease which was killing his heart and spirit. In a letter written to her at the end of July 1820, when he is smarting and writhing at the echoes of some light gossip which have reached him about this love which is shaking his life to its foundations, when he is worried by some misunderstanding on the part of Fanny, and tortured by incessant doubts of her loyalty, 'let me but be certain', he cries,

> 'that you are mine heart and soul, and I could die more happily than I could otherwise live. If you think me cruel—if you think I have sleighted you—do muse it over again and see into my heart. My love to you is "true as truth's simplicity and simpler than the infancy of truth" as I think I once said before.'

These are the lines marked by him at the end of Troilus' speech to Cressida, which expresses precisely his own feelings at this time: passionate love, mingled with a haunting suspicion, a premonition, that the object is not wholly worthy of it.

> O that I thought it could be in a woman:
> As if it can, I will presume in you,
> To feede for aye her lampe and flames of loue.
> To keepe her constancie in plight and youth,
> Out-liuing beauties outward, with a minde
> That doth renew swifter then blood decaies:

'Could I be convinced', continues Troilus, that my 'integrity and truth to you' were matched on your part with

>   such a winnowed purity in loue,
> How were I then vplifted!

Clearly he identifies himself all through with Troilus, reading with passionate, eager understanding, and much of the poignant interest of the markings in *Troilus and Cressida* here reprinted (pp. 149–78 below) is owing to the fact that he almost certainly underlines many passages primarily from that point of view. Such is the character of Troilus,

> Not yet mature, yet matchlesse, firme of word,
> Speaking in deedes, and deedelesse in his tongue;
> Not soone prouok't, nor being prouok't, soone calm'd;
> His heart and hand both open, and both free:

or his weak and helpless condition in the toils of love which he

describes in a series of vivid images in four lines at the beginning
of the play (I. i. 9–12), or his passionate reproach to Pandarus, who
might in this respect well be Brown, of his entire lack of comprehension of the quality of his love for Cressid. The wonderful
passage in Act III, Sc. ii, where Troilus describes his impatience and
dizziness of expectation,

> I stalke about her doore
> Like a strange soule upon the Stigian bankes
> Staying for waftage,

which Keats referred to when writing to George in October 1818,
is underlined completely (ll. 8–39), with an extra mark for the
simile used by Pandarus of Cressid fetching 'her breath so short
as a new tane Sparrow'.

Otherwise, throughout the play, he marks, as always, the images
or vivid phrases; in the Prologue, for instance, his sensitiveness
to sound aiding sense and helping to form a picture is worth
noting, as in

> . . . the deepe-drawing Barke do there disgorge
> Their warlike frautage:

or

> Now Expectation tickling skittish spirits;

so also the earlier part of the great third scene of Act I, a sweeping
torrent of imagery, greater in force and variety than anything else
even Shakespeare himself has ever approached, has almost every
line marked. Some of these are doubly or trebly marked, down the
side as well, such as

> The baby figure of the Gyant-masse
> Of things to come at large.

or the passage beginning

> Blunt wedges riue hard knots: the seeded Pride
> That hath to this maturity blowne up
> In ranke *Achilles,*

to which he adds the note 'One's very breath while leaning over

these pages is held for fear of blowing this line away—as easily
as the gentlest breeze Robs dandelions of their fleecy Crowns.' [1]
Among other lines doubly or trebly marked are

> ... almost like the gods,
> Doe thoughtes unuaile in their dumbe cradles:
> Crams his rich theeuerie up
> As many farewels as be stars in heauen.

Or a vivid touch of description, such as

> The large *Achilles* (on his prest-bed lolling)

has three side-marks as well as underlining, and indeed it may well
rank with the lines already quoted (p. 21 above) for its power of
calling up a whole picture by the use of one or two words. He has
underlined separately the rush of nouns and verbs in Ulysses' great
speech on order, '*degree, priority*, and *place*', '*divert* and *cracke, rend*
and *deracinate*', as if to emphasize the amazing mass and volume of
rhetoric which only Shakespeare could use without being weakened
by it; and Ulysses' second great speech, in which one image melts
into the other so quickly that we are left breathless following them,
has nearly every line marked.

The five notes to *Troilus* are of special interest. Two are on
textual points, one upholding the folio reading in I. i. 39,

> (as when the Sunne doth light a-scorne)

which, he says, the commentators have 'hocus pocus'd into "a
storm" thereby destroying the depth of the simile'; indeed, in view
of what Keats says, the modern reading seems much on a par with
Johnson's emendation of 'my *way* of life' into 'my *May* of Life'

> Is fall'n into the sear, the yellow leaf.

---

[1] It is interesting that Keats here seems to be quoting from a reminiscence of himself, an
affirmative form of a line in an intermediate stage in the beginning of *Hyperion*. The
present version :
> Not so much life as on a summer's day
> Robs not one light seed from the feather'd grass,
was added in the proof sheets, but in the Woodhouse transcript the last line reads
> Robs not at all the dandelion's fleece.
This would indicate that the note in *Troilus* was made possibly in Oct.–Nov. 1818 and
probably before April 1819, when the finished manuscript of *Hyperion* was sent to Woodhouse.

PLATE 19

Pan. You are such another.
Boy. Sir, my Lord would instantly speake with you.
Pan. Where?
Boy. At your owne house.
Pan. Good Boy tell him I come, I doubt he bee hurt.
Fare ye well good Neece.
Cres. Adieu Vnkle.
Pan. Ile be with you Neece by and by.
Cres. To bring Vnkle.
Pan. I, a token from Troylus.
Cres. By the same token, you are a Bawd. Exit Pand.
Words, vowes, gifts, teares, & loues full sacrifice,
He offers in anothers enterprise:
But more in Troylus thousand fold I see,
Then in the glasse of Pandar's praise may be;
Yet hold I off. Women are Angels wooing,
Things won are done, ioyes soule lyes in the dooing:
That she belou'd, knowes nought, that knowes not this;
Men prize the thing vngain'd, more then it is.
That she was neuer yet, that euer knew
Loue got so sweet, as when desire did sue:
Therefore this maxime out of loue I teach;
" Atchieuement, is command; vngain'd, beseech.
That though my hearts Contents firme loue doth beare,
Nothing of that shall from mine eyes appeare. Exit.

144

The gentle Thetis, and anon behold
The strong ribb'd Barke through liquid Mountaines cut,
Bounding betweene the two moyst Elements
Like Perseus Horse. Where's then the sawcy Boate,
Whose weake vntimber'd sides but euen now
Co-riual'd Greatnesse? Either to harbour fled,
Or made a Toste for Neptune. Euen so,
Doth valours shew, and valours worth diuide
In stormes of Fortune.
For, in her ray and brightnesse,
The Heard hath more annoyance by the Breeze
Then by the Tyger: But, when the splitting winde
Makes flexible the knees of knotted Oakes,
And Flies fled vnder shade, why then
The thing of Courage,
As rowz'd with rage, with rage doth sympatize,
And with an accent tun'd in selfe-same key,
Retyres to chiding Fortune.
Vlys. Agamemnon:
Thou great Commander, Nerue, and Bone of Greece,
Heart of our Numbers, soule, and onely spirit,
In whom the tempers, and the mindes of all
Should be shut vp: Heare what Vlysses speakes,
Besides the applause and approbation
The which most mighty for thy place and sway,

And

Note, in Keats's script, to *Troilus and Cressida* (I. iii. 13–17) in his folio edition

The other asks why

> Be shooke to ayrie ayre   (III. iii. 226)

of the folio should appear in modern versions as

> Be shook to air.

As Mr. Buxton Forman remarks, ' Echo answers why?'

The third note (see Plate 19) is appended to the passage in which Agamemnon expounds to the assembled princes how it is that all designs 'begun on earth below' fall short of expectation,

> Sith euery action that hath gone before,
> Whereof we haue Record, Triall did draw
> Bias and thwart, not answering the ayme:

Keats here, swift as a shaft of sunlight, gives us a sudden glimpse into the depth of his reverence for Shakespeare and boundless admiration of his genius, using for him the two adjectives supremely his when he speaks of his 'indolent and kingly gaze'. 'His plans of tasks to come', the note ends, ' were not of this world—if what he purposed to do hereafter would not in his own Idea "answer the aim" how tremendous must have been his Conception of Ultimates.'

We know that Keats was reading *King Lear* in the folio with intense absorption on January the 22nd 1818, for he writes to his brothers on the 23rd, 'I sat down yesterday to read "King Lear" once again: the thing appeared to demand the prologue of a sonnet, I wrote it, and began to read' (see Plate 20). The sonnet gives us a strange and vivid glimpse of what the reading of Shakespeare meant to Keats, especially the great tragedies; it was so intense and passionate an experience of the spirit, consuming, yet revivifying, that he had definitely to brace and prepare himself for it.

King Lear is very much marked; the greater number of Lear's speeches have every line underlined, and in addition he specially marks similes and metaphors,

> Which like an Engine, wrencht my frame of Nature
> From the fixt place:
>> thredding darke ey'd night;

epithets,

> those *Pelicane Daughters*
> His *nighted* life
> *elfe* all my haires in knots
> *eare-kissing arguments*
> *Milke-Liver'd man*
> *A most Toad-spotted Traitor*;

touches of character, such as Regan's order about the newly blinded Gloucester,

> Go thrust him out at gates, *and let him smell*
> *His way to Dover*,

or of pathos, as Lear's

> Deere daughter, I confesse that I am old;
> Age is vnnecessary:

or

> We two alone will sing like Birds i' th' Cage.

At the end of Act I, Sc. i, l. 291, when Goneril, turning to Regan, says

> You see how full of changes his age is,

Keats appends this note, which is itself, in form and intensity of feeling, a short prose poem:

'How finely is the brief of Lear's character sketched in this conference—from this point does Shakspeare spur him out to the mighty grapple—" the seeded pride that hath to this maturity blowne up" Shakspeare doth scatter abroad on the winds of Passion, where the germs take b[u]oyant root in stormy Air, suck lightning sap, and become voiced dragons—self-will and pride and wrath are taken at a rebound by his giant hand and mounted to the Clouds—there to remain and thunder eve[r]more.'

In I. v. 14, when Goneril has just cut down Lear's followers from a hundred to fifty, the Fool says:

> Shalt see thy other Daughter will vse thee kindly, for though she's as like this, as a Crabbe's like an Apple, yet I can tell what I can tell.

PLATE 20

FINIS.

On sitting down to read King Lear once again.

O Golden-tongued Romance, with serene lute!
Fair plumed Syren, Queen of far-away!
Leave melodizing on this wintry day,
Shut up thine olden Pages and be mute.
Adieu! for, once again, the fierce dispute,
Betwixt Damnation and impassion'd clay
Must I burn through; once more humbly assay
The bitter-sweet of this Shaksperean fruit.

Chief Poet! and ye Clouds of Albion,
Begetters of our deep eternal theme!
When through the old oak forest I am gone,
Let me not wander in a barren dream:
But, when I am consumed in the fire,
Give me new Phœnix wings to fly at my desire.

Jan'y 22. 1818.

Sonnet written by Keats on January 22, 1818, in his folio edition of Shakespeare, on a blank space at the end of *Hamlet* and facing the opening of *King Lear*

At this point Keats writes in Lear's pitiful words on turning again to Goneril after the 'tender-hefted' Regan has halved the fifty (II. iv. 262)

> Thy fifty yet doth double five and twenty.

The third note is to II. i. 96–9

> *Reg.* Was he not companion with the riotous Knights
>   That tended vpon my Father?
> *Glo.* I know not Madam, 'tis too bad, too bad.
> *Bast.* Yes Madam, he was of that consort.

'This bye-writing is more marvellous than the whole ripped up contents of Pernambuca—or any buca whatever—on the earth or in the waters under the earth.'

Keats is interested in the 'bye-writing' and specially marks the quick exchange of 'No' and 'Yes' between Lear and Kent (II. iv. 15–21), Cornwall and Gloucester's hurried words (II. iv. 298–300), and the talk between Kent, Lear, the Fool, and Gloucester in III. vi. 87–96.

It is clear from the marking throughout how strongly Keats felt the truth which he expressed more than once in various forms, and with special reference to this play in the letter to his brothers of the 28th of December, 1817:—

'The excellence of every art is its intensity, capable of making all disagreeables evaporate from their being in close relationship with Beauty and Truth. Examine "King Lear", and you will find this exemplified throughout'.

Keats's chief reading of *A Midsummer Night's Dream* was done in his small Shakespeare (Princeton copy), but in the folio he has marked again the passages which so pleased him in the speeches of Titania and Oberon in Act II, Sc. i (in many modern editions, following Pope, marked Sc. ii), ll. 81–164. The folio underlinings are not exactly the same as in the little book (printed below, pp. 90–2), but very nearly so. To the beginning of Titania's speech (II. i. 81)

> These are the forgeries of iealousie,
> And neuer since the middle Summers spring

Met we on hil, in dale, forrest, or mead,
By paued fountaine, or by rushie brooke,
Or in the beached margent of the sea,
To dance our ringlets to the whistling Winde,
But with thy braules thou hast disturb'd our sport.

he has written this long note:

'There is something exquisitely rich and luxurious in Titania's
saying "since the middle summer's spring" as if Bowers were
not exuberant and covert enough for fairy sports untill their
second sprouting—which is surely the most bounteous over-
whelming of all Nature's goodnesses. She steps forth benignly
in the spring and her conduct is so gracious that by degrees all
things are becoming happy under her wings and nestle against
her bosom: she feels this love and gratitude too much to remain
selfsame, and unable to contain herself buds forth the overflow-
ings of her heart about the middle summer. O Shakespeare thy
ways are but just searchable! The thing is a piece of profound
verdure.'

Romeo and Juliet is marked only up to Act III, Sc. ii, l. 29 (the
first thirteen pages in the folio), chiefly the scene in the orchard
(II. ii), where Romeo's speeches 2–12, 26–32, 164–6, and Juliet's
85–106, 112–15, 116–24, 131–5, 158–63, 176–81 are almost completely underlined; Romeo's passionate avowal to Friar Laurence
(I. vi. 3–8) is trebly scored; and many single lines are marked, such as:

That in Gold claspes, Lockes in the Golden storie:
Tickle the senselesse rushes with their heeles:
Temp'ring extremities with extreame sweete.
See how she leanes her cheeke vpon her hand.
What early tongue so sweet saluteth me?
Which to the high top gallant of my joy,
              the Sunnes beames,
Driuing backe shadowes ouer lowring hils.
Thei'le be in Scarlet straight at any newes.

Only the first eight pages of *Henry IV*, Part I, are marked, up to II. iii. 92. There is not very much underlined; Mortimer's encounter with Glendower (I. iii. 102–6), Worcester's and Hotspur's vivid images (I. iii. 188–93, 201–5), and the talk of the carriers (II. i. 11–20) are the longest speeches marked. Otherwise, chiefly single lines:

> where they did spend
A sad and bloody houre:

Charles waine is ouer the new Chimney,

> Indeede Ile breake
thy little finger *Harry*,

and epithets:

> Night-tripping-Faiery
> moody Frontier
> on the gentle Seuernes siedgie banke.

Keats could not well take with him the heavy folio volume on his last voyage on the *Maria Crowther*; he took the small edition of Shakespeare and the volume of the *Poems*; the folio he gave before he left to Fanny Brawne, writing in under his own name ' To F. B. 1820'. There could be no stronger proof of how greatly he prized it.

Such then are the chief markings and points of interest in these volumes, which were in Keats's possession and constantly with him during the greater part of his poetic life. Some of them, he has told us directly, were his ' comfort'; all of them, we know indirectly, were his inspiration, his source of content, of joy, and of wonder; and in them he has left us an authentic record of the passionate ardour and acute critical judgement with which he read and studied Shakespeare, and a clear glimpse of some portion of what Shakespeare meant to him.

Every mark in them is, therefore, precious and significant, for we recognize now that Keats and Shakespeare had a very unusual, a very close, and subtle relationship. They were alike in certain qualities of mind and of art, a fact of which Keats himself was fully aware, and in some of these qualities they are unique among English poets.

We also know now, and the study of these volumes helps us to the fuller realization of it, that of all the tribute and rare appreciation which his countrymen have rendered to him during the last hundred years, that which Keats himself would have prized above all else is the verdict given by another great English poet in answer to his modest yet entirely assured reflection, 'I think I shall be among the English poets after my death':—'He is; he is with Shakespeare'.

PARALLEL PASSAGES

THE following are some parallel passages illustrating various kinds of reminiscence of thought or verbal likeness between *The Tempest* and *A Midsummer Night's Dream* on the one hand, and *Endymion* on the other. All the Shakespearian passages are underlined by Keats in his edition, and those marked with an asterisk are doubly marked, down the side as well. The Shakespearian text is, of course, given as it reads in Keats's copy; this is important, note for instance 'sleep are made of' (*Endymion*, i. 749), a reminiscence of 'dreams are made of' (*The Tempest*, IV. i. 157), which is what he read, instead of the folio reading 'on', always now printed.

The Shakespearian line references given here and in the following sections are to the one-volume Oxford Shakespeare, as the lines in Keats's editions are not numbered.

Thy turfy mountains, where live nibbling sheep,   IV. i. 62.

. . . . you, whose pastime   V. i. 38.
Is to make midnight-mushrooms:

Who, with thy saffron wings, upon my flowers   IV. i. 78.
Diffusest honey drops, refreshing showers:
And with each end of thy blue bow dost crown
My bosky acres, and my unshrubb'd down,
Rich scarf to my proud earth; . . . . .

Full fathom five thy father lies;   I. ii. 394.
          Of his bones are coral made;

The ditty does remember my drown'd father: I. ii. 402.

. . the baseless fabrick of this vision,   IV. i. 151.
The cloud-capp'd towers, the gorgeous palaces,
The solemn temples, ...
. . . .
. . . .

. . . . we are such stuff
As dreams are made of, and our little life
Is rounded with a sleep.

. . . . I met her deity   IV. i. 92.
Cutting the clouds towards Paphos; and her son
Dove drawn with her.

. . . . . . ye, whose precious charge   i. 203.
Nibble their fill at ocean's very marge,

Are not our lowing heifers sleeker than   i. 214.
Night-swollen mushrooms?

. . . shaping visions all about my sight   i. 568.
Of colours, wings, and bursts of spangly light;

        . . . The wind out-blows   i. 627.
Her scarf into a fluttering pavillion;
'Tis blue, and over-spangled with a million
Of little eyes, ...

Who dives three fathoms where the waters run   i. 639.
Gurgling in beds of coral:

Old ditties sigh above their father's grave;   i. 788.

I watch and dote upon the silver lakes   i. 740.
Pictur'd in western cloudiness, that takes
The semblance of gold rocks and bright gold sands,
Islands, and creeks, and amber-fretted strands
With horses prancing o'er them, palaces
And towers of amethyst,— . . . . .
. . . .
. . . . The Morphean fount
Of that fine element that visions, dreams,
And fitful whims of sleep are made of,

        At these words upflew   ii. 579.
The impatient doves, uprose the floating car,
Up went the hum celestial.

. . . . so I charm'd their ears   IV. i. 178.
That, calf-like, they my lowing follow'd through
Tooth'd briers, sharp furzes, pricking goss, and thorns,
Which enter'd their frail shins: at last I left them
I' the filthy-mantled pool . . . . .
    [The last nine words are not underlined by Keats]

. . . . I'll break my staff,   V. i. 54.
Bury it certain fathoms in the earth,
And, deeper than did ever plummet sound,
I'll drown my book.

I'll seek him deeper than e'er plummet sounded,   III. iii. 101.

I pr'ythee, let me bring thee where crabs grow;   II. ii. 180.
And I, with my long nails, will dig thee pig-nuts;
. . . .
                        I'll bring thee
To clust'ring filberds and sometimes I'll get thee
Young sea-mells from the rock. . . . .

I'll show thee the best springs; I'll pluck thee berries;   II. ii. 173.
I'll fish for thee, and get thee wood enough.

*Spring come to you at the farthest,   IV. i. 114.
In the very end of harvest;

A mad-pursuing of the fog-born elf,   ii. 277.
Whose flitting lantern, through rude nettle-briar,
Cheats us into a swamp, into a fire,
Into the bosom of a hated thing.

Down, down, uncertain to what pleasant doom,   ii. 661.
Swift as a fathoming plummet down he fell
Through unknown things;

. . . where dark yew trees, ...   iv. 673.
Will drop their scarlet berry cups of dew.

Honey from out the gnarled hive I'll bring,   iv. 682.
And apples, wan with sweetness, gather thee,—
Cresses that grow where no man may them see,
And sorrel untorn by the dew-claw'd stag:

. . . . The rill,   iv. 691.
Thou haply mayst delight in, will I fill
With fairy fishes from the mountain tarn,
And thou shalt feed them from the squirrel's barn.

. . . . I will begin   i. 39.
. . . .
Now while the early budders are just new,

O may no wintry season, bare and hoary,   i. 54.
See it half-finish'd: but let Autumn bold,
With universal tinge of sober gold,
Be all about me when I make an end.

. . .   strange and several noises   V. i. 232.
Of roaring, shrieking, gingling chains,
And more diversity of sounds, . . .

[Even now we heard] a hollow burst of bellowing   II. i. 319.
Like bulls, or rather lions:

*Be not afeard; the isle is full of noises,   III. ii. 147.
Sounds, and sweet airs, that give delight, and hurt not.

All the infections that the sun sucks up   II. ii. 1.
From bogs, fens, flats, on Prosper fall, . . .

How lush and lusty the grass looks! how green!   II. i. 55.
. . The ground indeed is tawny.
. . With an eye of green in't.

*Sometimes a thousand twangling instruments   III. ii. 149.
Will hum about mine ears; . . .

Stage directions:

Music. Re-enter Ariel, invisible.   II. i. 305.

Enter Ariel, invisible, playing solemn Music.   II. i. 192.

Re-enter Ariel, invisible, playing and singing;   I. ii. 375.

Where should this music be? i' the air, or on the earth? I. ii. 385.
It sounds no more:—and, sure, it waits upon
Some god of the island. . . . .

*This is no mortal business, . . .   I. ii. 403.

Strange ministrant of undescribed sounds,   i. 285.
That come a swooning over hollow grounds,

. . . . . Breather round our farms,   i. 283.
To keep off mildews, and all weather harms:

. . . . . . And, as the year,   i. 45.
Grows lush in juicy stalks, . .

. . . . . fresh before me as the green   i. 38.
Of our own vallies:

. . . . . Have not rains   i. 216.
Green'd over April's lap?

. . the swift treble pipe, and humming string.   i. 314.

The quick invisible strings, ...   i. 500.
                [of Peona's lute]

This sleepy music, forc'd him walk tiptoe: ii. 358.
For it came more softly than the east could blow
Arion's magic to the Atlantic isles;

. . . . this   ii. 373.
Dew-dropping melody,

Stage direction:

Solemn and strange Music.	III. iii. 17.
Marvellous sweet music!	III. iii. 19.

                 Thou shalt be as free   I. ii. 495.
As mountain winds:

If by your art, my dearest father, you have   I. ii. 1–9.
Put the wild waters in this roar, allay them.
The sky, it seems, would pour down stinking pitch,
But that the sea, mounting to the welkin's cheek,
Dashes the fire out. O, I have suffer'd
With those that I saw suffer! A brave vessel,
Who had no doubt some noble creatures in her,
Dash'd all to pieces. O, the cry did knock
Against my very heart! Pour souls! they perish'd.

[Of the above passage only half line 8 and half 9 is underlined by Keats]

You sun-burn'd sicklemen, of August weary,   IV. i. 134.
Come hither from the furrow, and be merry:

A MIDSUMMER NIGHT'S DREAM

Quite over-canopied with lush woodbine,   II. i. 251.
With sweet musk-roses, and with eglantine:

*We, Hermia, ...   III. ii. 203.
Have with our neelds created both one flower,
Both on one sampler, sitting on one cushion,
Both warbling of one song, both in one key;

. . . hist, when the airy stress   i. 783.
Of music's kiss impregnates the free winds,

                              On a day,   iii. 645.
Sitting upon a rock above the spray,
I saw grow up from the horizon's brink
A gallant vessel: . . . . . .
. . . .
. . . . . not long, before arose
Dark clouds, and muttering of winds morose.
Old Æolus would stifle his mad spleen,
But could not: therefore all the billows green
Toss'd up the silver spume against the clouds.
The tempest came: I saw that vessel's shrouds
In perilous bustle; while upon the deck
Stood trembling creatures. I beheld the wreck;
The final gulphing; the poor struggling souls:
I heard their cries amid loud thunder-rolls.

A crowd of shepherds with as sunburnt looks   i. 139.
As may be read of in Arcadian books;

When last the sun his autumn tresses shook,   i. 440.
And the tann'd harvesters rich armfuls took.

. . . . . rain-scented eglantine   i. 100.
Gave temperate sweets to that well-wooing sun;

. . . . an arbour, overwove   i. 431.
By many a summer's silent fingering;
To whose cool bosom she was us'd to bring
Her playmates, with their needle broidery,
And minstrel memories of times gone by.

*. . . . . . in grove, or green,   II. i. 28.
By fountain clear, or spangled star-light sheen,

To-morrow night when Phœbe doth behold   I. i. 209.
Her silver visage in the wat'ry glass,
Decking with liquid pearl the bladed grass,
And that same dew which sometime on the buds   IV. i. 60.
Was wont to swell, like round and orient pearls,
Stood now within the pretty flowrets' eyes,
Like tears . . . . . .

My love shall hear the music of my hounds.—   IV. i. 112.
Uncouple in the western valley; . . .
We will, fair queen, up to the mountain's top,
And mark the musical confusion
Of hounds and echo in conjunction.
   [The last line is not underlined]
The skies, the fountains, every region near   IV. i. 122.
Seem'd all one mutual cry: . . . .
. . . . A cry more tuneable   IV. i. 130.
Was never holla'd to, nor cheer'd with horn.

*And pluck the wings from painted butterflies,   III. i. 179.
To fan the moon-beams from his sleeping eyes:

*And for night-tapers, crop their waxen thighs,   III. i. 176.
And light them at the fiery glow-worm's eyes,

[Cupid all arm'd:] . . . . .
* . . loos'd his love-shaft smartly from his bow,   II. i. 159.
As it should pierce a hundred thousand hearts:
But I might see young Cupid's fiery shaft
Quench'd in the chaste beams of the wat'ry moon,

Echoing grottos, full of tumbling waves   i. 459.
And moonlight; aye, to all the mazy world
Of silvery enchantment! . . . . .
. . bursts of spangly light;   i. 569.
. . over-spangled . . .   i. 629.

. . the pearliest dew not brings   i. 469.
Such morning incense from the fields of May,
As do those brighter drops that twinkling stray
From those kind eyes,— . . . .

. . No, I will once more raise   i. 477.
My voice upon the mountain-heights; once more
Make my horn parley from their foreheads hoar:
Again my trooping hounds their tongues shall loll
Around the breathed boar: . . .

. . . . . yet, his eyelids   i. 762.
Widened a little, as when Zephyr bids
A little breeze to creep between the fans
Of careless butterflies: . . . .

And, while beneath the evening's sleepy frown   ii. 140.
Glow-worms began to trim their starry lamps,

         O Cynthia, ten-times bright and fair!   ii. 170.
From thy blue throne, now filling all the air,
Glance but one little beam of temper'd light
Into my bosom, that the dreadful might
And tyranny of love be somewhat scar'd!

KEATS'S MARKINGS

THE following is an accurate reprint of all the marks, annotations, and underlinings in the text of four plays in Keats's small seven-volume edition of Shakespeare (Princeton copy): *The Tempest, A Midsummer Night's Dream, Measure for Measure,* and *Antony and Cleopatra*; also of those in *Troilus and Cressida* in his folio edition at Hampstead. The gaps between the extracts are indicated by the line references, which are to the one-volume Oxford Shakespeare.

THE TEMPEST

ACT I

SCENE I—*On a Ship at Sea. A Storm, with Thunder and Lightning*

I. i. 18.   *Boats.* <u>What care these roarers for the name of king?</u>

I. i. 58.   *Boats.* <u>What, must our mouths be cold?</u>

I. i. 62.   *Ant.*   'Would, thou might'st lie drowning,
<u>The washing of ten tides!</u>

SCENE II—*The Island: before the Cell of* PROSPERO

I. ii. 8.   *Mir.*   <u>O, the cry did knock</u>
<u>Against my very heart!</u>

I. ii. 26.   *Pros.* The direful spectacle of the wreck, which touch'd
<u>The very virtue of compassion</u> in thee,

I. ii. 49.   *Pros.*   What seest thou else
<u>In the dark backward and abysm of time?</u>

I. ii. 79.   *Pros.* Being once perfected how to grant suits,
How to deny them; whom to advance, and whom
To <u>trash for over-topping;</u> new created
The creatures that were mine; I say, or chang'd them,
| Or else new form'd them: having both the key
| Of officer and office, set all hearts
| To what tune pleas'd his ear; that now he was
| The ivy, which had hid my princely trunk,

| And suck'd my verdure out on 't.—Thou attend'st not:
| I pray thee, mark me.

I. ii. 99.   *Pros.*   like one,
* Who having, unto truth, by telling of it,
Made such a sinner of his memory,
To credit his own lie,—

I. ii. 108.   *Pros.*   he needs will be
Absolute Milan:

I. ii. 132.   *Pros.* Me, and thy crying self.

I. ii. 145.   *Pros.*   where they prepar'd
A rotten carcase of a boat, not rigg'd,
Nor tackle, sail, nor mast; the very rats
Instinctively had quit it: there they hoist us,
To cry to the sea that roar'd to us; to sigh
To the winds, whose pity, sighing back again,
Did us but loving wrong.
    Mir.   Alack! what trouble
Was I then to you!
    Pros.   O! a cherubim
Thou wast, that did preserve me! Thou didst smile,
Infused with a fortitude from heaven,
| When I have deck'd the sea with drops full salt;
Under my burden groan'd; which rais'd in me
An undergoing stomach, to bear up
Against what should ensue.

I. ii. 168. | *Mir.*   'Would I might
| But ever see that man!
    Pros.   Now I arise:—
Sit still, and hear the last of our sea-sorrow.

I. ii. 176.   *Mir.* (For still 'tis beating in my mind,)

I. ii. 180.   *Pros.*   and by my prescience
I find my zenith doth depend upon
A most auspicious star; whose influence

KEATS'S NOTE] * Who loving an untruth?

| If now I court not, but omit, my fortunes
| Will ever after droop.—Here cease more questions;
| Thou art inclined to sleep;

I. ii. 188. *Pros.* Approach, my Ariel; come.

I. ii. 190. *Ari.*   be 't to fly,
To swim, to dive into the fire, to ride
On the curl'd clouds; to thy strong bidding, task
| Ariel, and all his quality.

I. ii. 196. *Ari.* I boarded the king's ship; now on the beak,
Now in the waist, the deck, in every cabin,
I flam'd amazement: sometimes, I'd divide,
And burn in many places; on the top-mast,
The yards, and bowsprit, would I flame distinctly;
Then meet, and join: Jove's lightnings, the precursors
O' the dreadful thunder-claps, more momentary
And sight-outrunning were not: the fire, and cracks
Of sulphurous roaring, the most mighty Neptune
Seem'd to besiege, and make his bold waves tremble;
Yea, his dread trident shake.
          Pros.   My brave spirit!
Who was so firm, so constant, that this coil
Would not infect his reason?
          Ari.   Not a soul
But felt a fever of the mad, and play'd
Some tricks of desperation: all, but mariners,
Plung'd in the foaming brine, and quit the vessel,
Then all a-fire with me:

I. ii. 221. *Ari.* The king's son have I landed by himself;
‖Whom I left cooling of the air with sighs,
‖In an odd angle of the isle, and sitting,
‖His arms in this sad knot.

I. ii. 227. *Ari.*   in the deep nook, where once
Thou call'dst me up at midnight to fetch dew
From the still-vex'd Bermoothes, there she's hid:

I. ii. 246. *Ari.*   I pray thee
Remember, I have done thee worthy service;

Told thee no lies, made no mistakings, serv'd
Without or grudge or grumblings: thou didst promise
To bate me a full year.
  Pros.   Dost thou forget
From what a torment I did free thee?
  Ari.   No.
  Pros. Thou dost; and think'st
It much, to tread the ooze of the salt deep;
To run upon the sharp wind of the north;
To do me business in the veins o' the earth,
When it is bak'd with frost.
  Ari.   I do not, sir.
  Pros. Thou liest, malignant thing! Hast thou forgot
The foul witch Sycorax, who, with age, and envy,
Was grown into a hoop? hast thou forgot her?

I. ii. 272. *Pros.* And, for thou wast a spirit too delicate
To act her earthly and abhorr'd commands,
Refusing her grand hests, she did confine thee,
By help of her more potent ministers,
And in her most unmitigable rage,
Into a cloven pine; within which rift
Imprison'd, thou didst painfully remain
A dozen years; within which space she died,
And left thee there; where thou didst vent thy groans,
As fast as mill-wheels strike: then was this island
(Save for the son that she did litter here,
A freckled whelp hag-born), not honour'd with
A human shape.

I. ii. 285. *Pros.* Dull thing, I say so; . . . . .

I. ii. 291. . . . . . it was mine art,
When I arriv'd, and heard thee, that made gape
The pine, and let thee out.
  Ari.   I thank thee, master.
  Pros. If thou more murmur'st, I will rend an oak,
And peg thee in his knotty entrails, till
Thou hast howl'd away twelve winters.
  Ari.   Pardon, master:

I will be correspondent to command,
||| And do my spiriting gently.

I. ii. 300.   *Ari.* What shall I do? say what: what shall I do?
                Pros. Go make thyself like to a nymph o' the sea;

                Re-enter ARIEL, *like a Water-Nymph*
I. ii. 317.   *Pros.* Fine apparition! My quaint Ariel,
                Hark in thine ear.

I. ii. 321.   *Cal.* As wicked dew as e'er my mother brush'd
                With raven's feather from unwholesome fen,
                Drop on you both! a south-west blow on ye,
                And blister you all o'er!
                    Pros. For this, be sure, to-night thou shalt have cramps,
                Side-stitches, that shall pen thy breath up; urchins
                | Shall, for that vast of night that they may work,
                All exercise on thee: thou shalt be pinch'd
                | As thick as honeycombs, each pinch more stinging
                Than bees that made them.

I. ii. 332.   *Cal.*   When thou camest first,
                Thou strok'dst me, and mad'st much of me; would'st give me
                | Water with berries in 't; and teach me how
                | To name the bigger light, and how the less,
                That burn by day and night: and then I lov'd thee,
                And show'd thee all the qualities o' the isle,
                The fresh springs, brine-pits, barren place, and fertile;
                Cursed be I that did so!—All the charms
                Of Sycorax, toads, beetles, bats, light on you!
                For I am all the subjects that you have,
                Which first was mine own king; and here you sty me
                In this hard rock, whiles you do keep from me
                The rest of the island.

I. ii. 349.   *Cal.* O ho, O ho!—

I. ii. 356.   *Pros.*   but would'st gabble like
                A thing most brutish,

I. ii. 365.   *Pros.*   Hag-seed, hence!

I. ii. 367.   *Pros.*   Shrug'st thou, malice?

I. ii. 369.   *Pros.*   I'll rack thee with old cramps;
                Fill all thy bones with aches:

Re-enter ARIEL, *invisible, playing and singing;* FERDINAND *following him*

ARIEL'S SONG

I. ii. 375. | Come unto these yellow sands,
                | And then take hands:
                | Court'sied when you have, and kiss'd,
                | (The wild waves whist)
                | Foot it featly here and there;
                  And, sweet sprites, the burden bear.
                | Hark, hark!
                     Bur. Bowgh, wowgh.   [*Dispersedly.*
                | The watch-dogs bark:
                     Bur. Bowgh, wowgh.   [*Dispersedly.*
                         Hark, hark! I hear
                | The strain of strutting chanticlere,
                          Cry, Cock-a-doodle-doo.

          Fer. Where should this music be? i' the air, or the earth?
It sounds no more:—and sure, it waits upon
Some god of the island. Sitting on a bank,
Weeping again the king my father's wreck,
This music crept by me upon the waters;
Allaying both their fury, and my passion,
With its sweet air: thence I have follow'd it,
Or it hath drawn me rather:—But 'tis gone.
No, it begins again.

ARIEL *sings.*

Full fathom five thy father lies;
    Of his bones are coral made;
Those are pearls that were his eyes:
    Nothing of him that doth fade,
But doth suffer a sea-change
Into something rich and strange.
Sea-nymphs hourly ring his knell:
Hark! now I hear them,—ding-dong, bell.
                Burden, ding-dong.

Fer. The ditty does remember my drown'd father:—
| This is no mortal business, nor no sound
That the earth owes:—I hear it now above me.
　　Pros. The fringed curtains of thine eye advance
And say, what thou seest yond'.
　　　Mir.　　　　　　　　　　What is 't? a spirit?
Lord, how it looks about! Believe me, sir,
It carries a brave form:—But 'tis a spirit.

I. ii. 417.　　*Pros.*　　　　　　Spirit, fine spirit! ..

I. ii. 418.　　*Fer.*　　　　　　Most sure, the goddess
On whom these airs attend!— . . . .

I. ii. 421.　　And that you will some good instruction give,
How I may bear me here:

I. ii. 432.　　*Fer.* Who with mine eyes, ne'er since at ebb,

I. ii. 437.　　*Pros.*　　　　　　At the first sight
They have chang'd eyes:—Delicate Ariel,
I 'll set thee free for this!

I. ii. 454.　　*Mir.* There 's nothing ill can dwell in such a temple:
If the ill spirit have so fair an house,
Good things will strive to dwell with 't.

l. ii. 459.　　*Pros.* Sea-water shalt thou drink, thy food shall be
The fresh-brook muscles, wither'd roots, and husks,
Wherein the acorn cradled. Follow.

I. ii. 471.　　*Pros.* Hence; hang not on my garments.

I. ii. 478.　| *Mir.*　　　　　　　　My affections
| Are then most humble; I have no ambition
| To see a goodlier man.

I. ii. 483.　| *Fer.* My spirits, as in a dream, are all bound up.
| My father's loss, the weakness which I feel,
| The wreck of all my friends, or this man's threats,
| To whom I am subdued, are but light to me,
| Might I but through my prison, once a day,

| Behold this maid: <u>all corners else o' the earth</u>
| <u>Let liberty make use of;</u>

I. ii. 491.   *Pros.*   fine <u>Ariel</u>!

I. ii. 495.   *Pros.*   <u>Thou shalt be as free</u>
As <u>mountain winds:</u>

ACT II

SCENE I—*Another Part of the Island*

II. i. 42.   *Adr.* It must needs be of <u>subtle, tender, and delicate temperance.</u>

II. i. 48.   *Adr.* <u>The air breathes upon us here most sweetly.</u>

II. i. 55.   *Gon.* How lush and lusty the grass looks! <u>how green!</u>
               Ant. <u>The ground, indeed, is tawny.</u>
               Seb. <u>With an eye of green in 't.</u>

II. i. 113.   *Alon.* <u>You cram these words into mine ears, against</u>
<u>The stomach of my sense:</u>

II. i. 121.   *Fran.* <u>I saw him beat the surges under him,</u>
<u>And ride upon their backs; he trod the water,</u>
<u>Whose enmity he flung aside, and breasted</u>
<u>The surge most swoln that met him: his bold head</u>
<u>'Bove the contentious waves he kept, and oar'd</u>
<u>Himself with his good arms in lusty stroke</u>
<u>To the shore, that o'er his wave-worn basis bow'd</u>
<u>As stooping to relieve him.</u> I not doubt,
He came alive to land.

II. i. 136.   *Seb.*   <u>and the fair soul herself</u>
<u>Weigh'd, between lothness and obedience, at</u>
<u>Which end o' the beam she'd bow.</u>

II. i. 189. | *Gon.* You are gentlemen of brave mettle: you would <u>lift the</u>
           | <u>moon out of her sphere,</u> if she would continue in it five <u>weeks</u>
           | without changing.

Enter ARIEL, *invisible, playing solemn Music*

II. i. 199.   *Alon.* What, all so soon asleep! <u>I wish mine eyes</u>
<u>Would, with themselves, shut up my thoughts:</u>

II. i. 201.   *Seb.*   Please you, sir,
Do not omit the <u>heavy offer of it</u>:

II. i. 216.   *Ant.* <u>My strong imagination</u>

II. i. 225. | *Seb.*   Thou dost snore distinctly;
| There 's meaning in thy snores.
        Ant. I am more serious than my custom: you
Must be so too, if heed me; which to do,
Trebles thee o'er.
 | *Seb.*   Well; I am standing water.
 | *Ant.* I 'll teach you how to flow.
 | *Seb.*   Do so: to ebb,
Hereditary sloth instructs me.

II. i. 234.   *Ant.*   <u>Ebbing men, indeed,</u>
<u>Most often do so near the bottom run,</u>
<u>By their own fear, or sloth.</u>
        Seb.   Pr'ythee, say on:
<u>The setting of thine eye, and cheek, proclaim</u>
<u>A matter from thee; and a birth, indeed,</u>
<u>Which throes thee much to yield.</u>

II. i. 293.   *Ant.* <u>To the perpetual wink</u>

II. i. 296.   *Ant.* <u>They 'll take suggestion, as a cat laps milk</u>;

Music. Re-enter ARIEL, *invisible*

II. i. 318.   *Seb.* Whiles we stood here securing your repose,
Even now, we heard a <u>hollow burst of bellowing</u>
<u>Like bulls, or rather lions</u>:

SCENE II—*Another Part of the Island*

Enter CALIBAN *with a Burden of Wood. A Noise of Thunder heard*

II. ii. 1.   *Cal.* <u>All the infections that the sun sucks up</u>
<u>From bogs, fens, flats, on Prosper fall, and make him</u>
<u>By inch-meal a disease</u>! His spirits hear me,
And yet I needs must curse. But <u>they 'll nor pinch,</u>
<u>Fright me with urchin shows, pitch me i' the mire,</u>
<u>Nor lead me, like a firebrand, in the dark,</u>

Out of my way, unless he bid them; but
For every trifle are they set upon me:
Sometimes like apes, that moe and chatter at me,
And after, bite me; then like hedge-hogs, which
Lie tumbling in my bare-foot way, and mount
Their pricks at my foot-fall; sometime am I
All wound with adders, who, with cloven tongues,
Do hiss me into madness:—Lo! now! lo!

Enter TRINCULO

II. ii. 20.   *Trin.* I hear it sing i' the wind: yond' same black cloud, yond'
huge one, looks like a foul bumbard that would shed his liquor.

II. ii. 43.   . . . I will here shroud, till the dregs of the storm be past.

II. ii. 85.   *Cal.* Thou dost me yet but little hurt; thou wilt
Anon, I know it by thy trembling;
Now Prosper works upon thee.

II. ii. 125.   *Cal.* These be fine things, an if they be not sprites.
That 's a brave god, and bears celestial liquor:

II. ii. 150.   *Cal.* I have seen thee in her, and I do adore thee;
My mistress showed me thee, thy dog, and bush.

II. ii. 160.   *Cal.* I 'll show thee every fertile inch o' the island;

II. ii. 173.   *Cal.* I 'll show thee the best springs; I 'll pluck thee berries;
I 'll fish for thee, and get thee wood enough.

II. ii. 180.   *Cal.* I pr'ythee, let me bring thee where crabs grow;
And I, with my long nails, will dig thee pig-nuts;
Show thee a jay's nest, and instruct thee how
To snare the nimble marmozet; I 'll bring thee
To clust'ring filberds, and sometimes I 'll get thee
Young sea-mells from the rock.

II. ii. 193. | *Cal.* No more dams I 'll make for fish;
                | Nor fetch in firing
                | At requiring,

| Nor scrape trenchering, nor wash dish;
| 'Ban, 'Ban, Ca-Caliban,
| Has a new master—Get a new man.

ACT III

Scene I—*Before Prospero's Cell*

III. i. 18.   *Mir.*   when this burns,
'Twill weep for having wearied you.

III. i. 31.   *Pros.*   Poor worm! thou art infected;

III. i. 34.   *Fer.*   I do beseech you
(Chiefly, that I might set it in my prayers,)
What is your name?

III. i. 39.   *Fer.*   Full many a lady
I have ey'd with best regard; and many a time
The harmony of their tongues hath into bondage
Brought my too diligent ear: for several virtues
Have I lik'd several women; never any
With so full soul, but some defect in her
Did quarrel with the noblest grace she ow'd,
And put it to the foil:

III. i. 73.   *Mir.*   I am a fool,
To weep at what I am glad of.

III. i. 80.   *Mir.* And all the more it seeks to hide itself,
The bigger bulk it shows.

Scene II—*Another Part of the Island*

III. ii. 35.   *Cal.* Lo, how he mocks me! wilt thou let him, my lord?

III. ii. 39.   *Cal.* Lo, lo, again! bite him to death, I pr'ythee.

Enter Ariel, *invisible*

III. ii. 76.   *Cal.*   for I'll not show him
Where the quick freshes are.

III. ii. 93.   *Cal.* Ha, ha, ha!

III. ii. 96.   *Cal.* Beat him enough: after a little time,
          I 'll beat him too.
              Ste.   Stand further.—Come, proceed.
      | *Cal.* Why, as I told thee, 'tis a custom with him
      | I' the afternoon to sleep: there thou may'st brain him,
      | Having first seiz'd his books; or with a log
      | Batter his skull, or paunch him with a stake,
      | Or cut his wezand with thy knife: Remember,
        First to possess his books; for without them
      | He 's but a sot, as I am, nor hath not
      | One spirit to command: They all do hate him,
        As rootedly as I: Burn but his books;
      | He has brave utensils (for so he calls them,)
      | Which, when he has a house, he 'll deck withal.
      | And that most deeply to consider, is
      | The beauty of his daughter; he himself
      | Calls her a nonpareil: I ne'er saw woman,
      | But only Sycorax my dam, and she;
      | But she as far surpasseth Sycorax,
      | As greatest does least.

III. ii. 118.   *Ste.*   (save our graces!)

III. ii. 128.   *Cal.* Thou mak'st me merry: I am full of pleasure;
          Let us be jocund: Will you troll the catch
          You taught me but while-ere?

                          [*Ariel plays the Tune on a Tabor and Pipe.*

III. ii. 147. ‖   *Cal.* Be not afeard; the isle is full of noises,
          Sounds, and sweet airs, that give delight, and hurt not.
          Sometimes a thousand twangling instruments
          Will hum about mine ears; and sometimes voices,
          That, if I then had wak'd after long sleep,
          Will make me sleep again: and then, in dreaming,
          The clouds, methought, would open, and show riches
          Ready to drop upon me; that, when I wak'd,
          I cry'd to dream again.

Scene III—*Another Part of the Island*

Solemn and strange Music;
and Prospero *above, invisible. Enter several strange Shapes,*
bringing in a Banquet; they dance about it with gentle Actions
of Salutation; and inviting the King, etc. to eat, they depart.

III. iii. 19.   *Gon.* Marvellous sweet music!
                  Alon. Give us kind keepers, heavens!

III. iii. 32.   *Gon.* Their manners are more gentle-kind, than of
                  Our human generation

III. iii. 40.   *Fran.* They vanish'd strangely.

Thunder and Lightning. Enter Ariel *like a Harpy: claps his*
      Wings upon the Table, and, with a quaint Device, the Banquet
      vanishes

III. iii. 55.   *Ari.*   the never-surfeited sea
                  Hath caused to belch up; . . . . . .

III. iii. 61.   . . . .   the elements
                  Of whom your swords are temper'd, may as well
                  Wound the loud winds, or with bemock'd-at stabs
                  Kill the still-closing waters, as diminish
                  One dowle that's in my plume; my fellow-ministers
                  Are like invulnerable. . . . . .

III. iii. 77.   Lingering perdition, (worse than any death
                  Can be at once,) shall step by step attend
                  You and your ways; . . . . .

III. iii. 81.   . . . . . . —is nothing, but heart's sorrow,
                  And a clear life ensuing.

He vanishes in Thunder: then, to soft Music, enter the Shapes again,
      and dance with Mops and Mowes, and carry out the Table

III. iii. 83.   *Pros.* Bravely the figure of this harpy hast thou
                  Perform'd, my Ariel; a grace it had, devouring:

III. iii. 96.   *Alon.* Methought, the billows spoke, and told me of it;
                  The winds did sing it to me; and the thunder,

That deep and dreadful organ-pipe, pronounc'd
The name of Prospero; it did bass my trespass.
Therefore my son i' the ooze is bedded; and
I 'll seek him deeper than e'er plummet sounded,
And with him there lie mudded.   [*Exit.*

III. iii. 105.   *Gon.* Like poison given to work a great time after,
Now 'gins to bite the spirits:—

ACT IV

Scene I—*Before* Prospero's *Cell*

IV. i. 20.   *Pros.* Sour-ey'd disdain,

IV. i. 23.   *Fer.*   As I hope
For quiet days, fair issue, and long life,

Enter Ariel

IV. i. 39.   *Pros.*   for I must
Bestow upon the eyes of this young couple
Some vanity of mine art;

IV. i. 44.   *Ari.* Before you can say, *Come,* and *go,*
          And breathe twice; and cry, *so, so;*
          Each one tripping on his toe,
          Will be here with mop and mowe:
          Do you love me, master? no.
    Pros. Dearly, my delicate Ariel:

IV. i. 51.   *Pros.*   do not give dalliance
Too much the rein; the strongest oaths are straw
To the fire i' the blood:

IV. i. 58.   *Pros.*   appear, and pertly.—
No tongue; all eyes; be silent.   [*Soft Music.*

IV. i. 60.   *Iris.* Ceres, most bounteous lady, thy rich leas
Of wheat, rye, barley, vetches, oats and pease;
Thy turfy mountains, where live nibbling sheep,
And flat meads thatch'd with stover, them to keep;
Thy banks with peonied and lilied brims,
Which spongy April at thy hest betrims,

To make cold nymphs chaste crowns; and thy broom-groves,
Whose shadow the dismissed bachelor loves,
Being lass-lorn; thy pole-clipt vineyard;
And thy sea-marge, steril, and rocky-hard,
Where thou thyself dost air: The queen o' the sky,
Whose watery arch, and messenger, am I,

IV. i. 78.   *Cer.* Who, with thy saffron wings, upon my flowers
Diffusest honey-drops, refreshing showers:
And with each end of thy blue bow dost crown
My bosky acres, and my unshrubb'd down,
Rich scarf to my proud earth; Why hath thy queen
Summon'd me hither, to this short-grass'd green?

IV. i. 92.   *Iris.*   I met her deity
Cutting the clouds towards Paphos; and her son
Dove-drawn with her:

SONG

IV. i. 106.   *Juno.* Honour, riches, marriage-blessing,
Long continuance, and increasing,
Hourly joys be still upon you!
Juno sings her blessings on you.

Cer. Earth's increase and foison plenty;
Barns, and garners never empty;
Vines, with clust'ring bunches growing;
Plants, with goodly burden bowing;
Spring come to you, at the farthest,
In the very end of harvest;
Scarcity, and want, shall shun you;
Ceres' blessing so is on you.

Fer. This is a most majestic vision, and
* Harmonious charmingly: May I be bold
To think these spirits?

IV. i. 128.   *Iris.* You nymphs, call'd Naiads, of the wand'ring brooks,
With your sedg'd crowns, and ever-harmless looks,

IV. i. 132.   *Iris.* Come, temperate nymphs,

KEATS'S NOTE] * Harmonises?

Enter certain Nymphs

IV. i. 134.   *Iris*. You sun-burn'd sicklemen, of August weary,
Come hither from the furrow, and be merry;
Make holy-day: your rye-straw hats put on,
And these fresh nymphs encounter every one
In country footing.

*Enter certain Reapers, properly habited; they join with the Nymphs
in a graceful Dance; towards the End whereof* PROSPERO
*starts suddenly, and speaks; after which, to a strange, hollow,
and confused Noise, they heavily vanish*

IV. i. 144.   *Mir*.   Never till this day,
Saw I him touch'd with anger so distemper'd.

IV. i. 148.   *Pros*.   These our actors,
As I foretold you, were all spirits, and
Are melted into air, into thin air:
And, like the baseless fabrick of this vision,
The cloud-capp'd towers, the gorgeous palaces,
The solemn temples, the great globe itself,
Yea, all which it inherit, shall dissolve;
And, like this insubstantial pageant faded,
Leave not a rack behind: we are such stuff
As dreams are made of, and our little life
Is rounded with a sleep.—Sir, I am vex'd;
Bear with my weakness; my old brain is troubled.
Be not disturb'd with my infirmity;
If you be pleas'd, retire into my cell,
And there repose; a turn or two I'll walk
‖ To still my beating mind.

Enter ARIEL

IV. i. 165.   *Ari*. Thy thoughts I cleave to;

IV. i. 167.   *Ari*. Ay, my commander: when I presented Ceres,
I thought to have told thee of it: but I fear'd,
Lest I might anger thee.

IV. i. 172.   *Ari*. So full of valour, that they smote the air
For breathing in their faces; beat the ground

For kissing of their feet: yet always bending
Towards their project: Then I beat my tabor,
At which, like unback'd colts, they prick'd their ears,
Advanc'd their eye-lids, lifted up their noses,
As they smelt music; so I charm'd their ears,
That, calf-like, they my lowing follow'd, through
Tooth'd briers, sharp furzes, pricking goss, and thorns,
Which enter'd their frail shins:

IV. i. 191. *Pros.* And as, with age, his body uglier grows,
So his mind cankers:

IV. i. 194. *Cal.* Pray you, tread softly, that the blind mole may not
Hear a foot fall:

IV. i. 206. *Cal.* Shall hood-wink this mischance:

IV. i. 218. *Cal.* Do that good mischief, which may make this island
Thine own for ever, and I, thy Caliban,
For aye thy foot-licker.
        Ste. Give me thy hand: I do begin to have bloody thoughts.

IV. i. 232. *Cal.* The dropsy drown this fool! . . . . .
IV. i. 234. . . . . if he awake,
From toe to crown he 'll fill our skins with pinches;
Make us strange stuff.

IV. i. 250. *Cal.*   we shall lose our time,
And all be turn'd to barnacles, or to apes
With foreheads villainous low.

        *A Noise of Hunters heard. Enter divers Spirits, in Shape of
                Hounds, and hunt them about;* PROSPERO *and* ARIEL *setting
                them on*

IV. i. 261. *Pros.* Go, charge my goblins that they grind their joints
With dry convulsions; shorten up their sinews
With aged cramps; and more pinch-spotted make them,
Than pard, or cat o' mountain.
        Ari.   Hark, they roar.
        Pros. Let them be hunted soundly: At this hour

Lie at my mercy all mine enemies;
Shortly shall all my labours end, and thou
Shalt have the air at freedom: for a little,
Follow, and do me service.   [*Exeunt.*

ACT V

SCENE I—*Before the Cell of* PROSPERO

V. i. 10.   *Ari.* In the lime-grove which weather-fends your cell;

V. i. 14.   Brim-full of sorrow, ...

V. i. 16.   His tears run down his beard, like winter's drops
From eaves of reeds: your charm so strongly works them,
That if you now beheld them, your affections
Would become tender.
     Pros.   Dost thou think so, spirit?
     Ari. Mine would, sir, were I human.
     Pros.   And mine shall.
Hast thou, which art but air, a touch, a feeling
Of their afflictions; . . . .

V. i. 27.   . . . . the rarer action is
In virtue than in vengeance:

V. i. 33.   *Pros.* Ye elves of hills, brooks, standing lakes, and groves;
And ye, that on the sands with printless foot
Do chase the ebbing Neptune, and do fly him,
When he comes back; you demy-puppets, that
By moon-shine do the green-sour ringlets make,
Whereof the ewe not bites; and you, whose pastime
Is to make midnight-mushrooms; that rejoice
To hear the solemn curfew; by whose aid
(Weak masters though ye be,) I have be-dimm'd
The noon-tide sun, call'd forth the mutinous winds,
And 'twixt the green sea and the azur'd vault
Set roaring war: to the dread rattling thunder
Have I given fire, and rifted Jove's stout oak
With his own bolt: the strong-bas'd promontory
Have I made shake; and by the spurs pluck'd up
The pine and cedar: . . . .

V. i. 51.   . . . . and, when I have requir'd
Some heavenly music (which even now I do,)
To work mine end upon their senses, that
This airy charm is for, I 'll break my staff,
Bury it certain fathoms in the earth,
And, deeper than did ever plummet sound,
I 'll drown my book.   [*Solemn Music.*

Re-enter ARIEL: *after him,* ALONSO, *with a frantic Gesture, attended
by* GONZALO; SEBASTIAN *and* ANTONIO *in like manner,
attended by* ADRIAN *and* FRANCISCO: *They all enter the Circle
which* PROSPERO *had made, and there stand charmed; which*
PROSPERO *observing, speaks*

A solemn air, and the best comforter
To an unsettled fancy, cure thy brains,
              . . . .

V. i. 63.   Mine eyes, even sociable to the show of thine,
Fall fellowly drops.—The charm dissolves apace;
And as the morning steals upon the night,
Melting the darkness, so their rising senses
Begin to chase the ignorant fumes that mantle
Their clearer reason.— . . . . . .

V. i. 79.   . . . . Their understanding
Begins to swell: and the approaching tide
Will shortly fill the reasonable shores,
That now lie foul and muddy.

ARIEL *re-enters, singing, and helps to attire* PROSPERO

V. i. 88.   Where the bee sucks, there suck I;
              In a cowslip's bell I lie:
              There I couch when owls do cry.
              On the bat's back I do fly,
              After summer, merrily:
       Merrily, merrily, shall I live now,
       Under the blossom that hangs on the bough.

Pros. Why, that 's my dainty Ariel; I shall miss thee,
But yet thou shalt have freedom:

V. i. 102.   *Ari.* I drink the air before me, and return
Or e'er your pulse twice beat.

V. i. 123.   *Pros.*   You do yet taste
Some subtilties o' the isle,

V. i. 151.   *Alon.*   mudded in that oozy bed
Where my son lies.

V. i. 153.   *Pros.*   I perceive, these lords
At this encounter do so much admire,
That they devour their reason; and scarce think
Their eyes do offices of truth, their words
Are natural breath: but howsoe'er you have
Been justled from your senses, ...

V. i. 163.   For 'tis a chronicle of day by day,

The Entrance of the Cell opens, and discovers FERDINAND *and* MIRANDA,
playing at Chess

V. i. 183.   *Mir.* How beauteous mankind is! O brave new world,
That has such people in 't!

Re-enter ARIEL, *with the* Master *and* Boatswain *amazedly following*

V. i. 226.   *Pros.* [*Aside to Ari.*] My tricksy spirit!

V. i. 232.   *Boats.* Where, but even now, with strange and several noises
Of roaring, shrieking, howling, gingling chains,
And more diversity of sounds, all horrible,
We were awak'd; strait-way, at liberty;
Where we, in all her trim, freshly beheld
Our royal, good, and gallant ship; our master
Cap'ring to eye her: On a trice, so please you,
Even in a dream, were we divided from them,
And were brought moping hither.
    Ari. Was 't well done?   ⎫
    Pros. Bravely, my diligence. ⎬ [*Aside*
                       ⎭

V. i. 246.   *Pros.* Do not infest your mind with beating on
The strangeness of this business;

Re-enter ARIEL, *driving in* CALIBAN, STEPHANO *and* TRINCULO, *in
their stolen Apparel*

V. i. 261.   *Cal.* O Setebos, these be brave spirits, indeed!

How fine my master is! I am afraid
He will chastise me.

V. i. 269.   *Pros.* His mother was a witch; and one so strong
That could control the moon, make flows and ebbs,
And deal in her command, without her power:

V. i. 276.   *Cal.*   I shall be pinch'd to death.

V. i. 295.   *Cal.*   What a thrice-double ass
Was I, to take this drunkard for a god,
And worship this dull fool!

V. i. 311.   *Pros.* Every third thought shall be my grave.

V. i. 314.   *Pros.* And promise you calm seas, auspicious gales,
And sail so expeditious, that shall catch
Your royal fleet far off.—My Ariel;—chick,—
That is thy charge; then to the elements
Be free, and fare thou well!—[*Aside.*] Please you draw near.
                                                    [*Exeunt.*

A MIDSUMMER NIGHT'S DREAM

ACT I

SCENE I—*Athens. A Room in the Palace of* THESEUS

I. i. 7. | *Hip.* Four days will quickly steep themselves in nights.
| Four nights will quickly dream away the time;
| And then the moon, like to a silver bow
| New bent in heaven, shall behold the night
| Of our solemnities.
      The.   Go, Philostrate,
Stir up the Athenian youth to merriments;
Awake the pert and nimble spirit of mirth;

I. i. 28. | *Ege.* Thou, thou, Lysander, thou hast given her rhymes,
| And interchang'd love-tokens with my child:
| Thou hast by moonlight at her window sung,
| With feigning voice, verses of feigning love;
| And stol'n the impression of her fantasy
With bracelets of thy hair, rings, gawds, conceits,
Knacks, trifles, nosegays, sweetmeats; messengers,
Of strong prevailment in unharden'd youth:

I. i. 71.   *The.* For aye to be in shady cloister mew'd,
To live a barren sister all your life,
Chanting faint hymns to the cold fruitless moon.
Thrice blessed they, that master so their blood,
To undergo such maiden pilgrimage:
But earthlier happy is the rose distill'd,
Than that, which, withering on the virgin thorn,
Grows, lives, and dies, in single blessedness.

I. i. 132.   *Lys.* Ah me! for aught that I could ever read,
| Could ever hear by tale or history,
| The course of true love never did run smooth:
| But, either it was different in blood;

I. i. 141.   *Lys.* Or, if there were a sympathy in choice,
| War, death, or sickness did lay siege to it:
Making it momentary as a sound,
| Swift as a shadow, short as any dream;

Brief as the lightning in the collied night,
| That, in a spleen, unfolds both heaven and earth,
| And ere a man hath power to say,—Behold!
The jaws of darkness do devour it up:
| So quick bright things come to confusion.
    Her. If then true lovers have been ever cross'd,
| It stands as an edict in destiny:
| Then let us teach our trial patience,
| Because it is a customary cross;
| As due to love, as thoughts, and dreams, and sighs,
| Wishes, and tears, poor fancy's followers.

I. i. 165.
    Lys. And in the wood, a league without the town,
Where I did meet thee once with Helena,
To do observance to a morn of May,
There will I stay for thee.

I. i. 171.
    Her. By the simplicity of Venus' doves:

I. i. 182.
    Hel.   O happy fair!
Your eyes are lode-stars; and your tongue's sweet air
More tunable than lark to shepherd's ear,
When wheat is green, when hawthorn buds appear,

I. i. 209.
    Lys. To-morrow night when Phœbe doth behold
Her silver visage in the wat'ry glass,
Decking with liquid pearl the bladed grass,
(A time that lovers' flights doth still conceal,)
Through Athens' gates have we devis'd to steal.
    Her. And in the wood, where often you and I
Upon faint primrose-beds were wont to lie,
Emptying our bosoms of their counsel sweet:
There my Lysander and myself shall meet;

ACT II

Scene I—*A Wood near Athens*

II. i. 6.
    Fai. I do wander every where,
Swifter than the moones sphere;
And I serve the fairy queen,
To dew her orbs upon the green:

The cowslips tall her pensioners be;
In their gold coats spots you see;
Those be rubies, fairy favours,
In those freckles live their savours:
I must go seek some dew-drops here,
And hang a pearl in every cowslip's ear.

II. i. 18.   *Puck.* The king doth keep his revels here to-night:
| Take heed, the queen come not within his sight.
| For Oberon is passing fell and wrath,
| Because that she, as her attendant, hath
A lovely boy, stol'n from an Indian king;
| She never had so sweet a changeling:
| And jealous Oberon would have the child
| Knight of his train, to trace the forests wild:
But she, perforce, withholds the loved boy,
| Crowns him with flowers, and makes him all her joy:
| And now they never meet in grove, or green,
| By fountain clear, or spangled star-light sheen,
| But they do square; that all their elves, for fear,
Creep into acorn cups, and hide them there.
        Fai. Either I mistake your shape and making quite,
Or else you are that shrewd and knavish sprite,
| Call'd Robin Goodfellow: are you not he,
| That fright the maidens of the villagery;
| Skim milk; and sometimes labour in the quern,
| And bootless make the breathless housewife churn;
| And sometime make the drink to bear no barm;
| Mislead night-wanderers, laughing at their harm:
| Those that Hobgoblin call you, and sweet Puck,
| You do their work, and they shall have good luck:
| Are not you he?
| *Puck.*   Thou speak'st aright;
| I am that merry wanderer of the night.
| I jest to Oberon, and make him smile,
| When I a fat and bean-fed horse beguile,
| Neighing in likeness of a filly foal:
| And sometime lurk I in a gossip's bowl,
| In very likeness of a roasted crab;
| And, when she drinks, against her lips I bob,

| And on her wither'd dew-lap pour the ale.
| The wisest aunt, telling the saddest tale,
| Sometime for three-foot stool mistaketh me:
| Then slip I from her bum, down topples she,
| And *tailor* cries, and falls into a cough;
| And then the whole quire hold their hips, and loffe;
| And waxen in their mirth, and neeze, and swear
| A merrier hour was never wasted there.—

Scene II

II. i. 64. *Tita.* Then I must be thy lady: But I know
When thou hast stol'n away from fairy land,
And in the shape of Corin sat all day,
Playing on pipes of corn, and versing love
To amorous Phillida. Why art thou here,
Come from the farthest steep of India?

II. i. 77. *Obe.* Didst thou not lead him through the glimmering night
From Perigenia, whom he ravished?
And make him with fair Ægle break his faith,
With Ariadne and Antiopa?
  Tita. These are the forgeries of jealousy:
And never, since the middle summer's spring,
Met we on hill, in dale, forest, or mead,
By paved fountain, or by rushy brook,
Or on the beachy margent of the sea,
To dance our ringlets to the whistling wind,
But with thy brawls thou hast disturb'd our sport.
Therefore the winds, piping to us in vain,
As in revenge, have suck'd up from the sea
Contagious fogs; which falling in the land,
Have every pelting river made so proud,
That they have overborne their continents:
The ox hath therefore stretch'd his yoke in vain,
| The ploughman lost his sweat; and the green corn
| Hath rotted, ere his youth attain'd a beard:
| The fold stands empty in the drowned field,
| And crows are fatted with the murrain flock;
| The nine men's morris is fill'd up with mud;
| And the quaint mazes in the wanton green

II. i. 100. | For lack of tread, are undistinguishable:
| The human mortals want their winter here;
| No night is now with hymn or carol blest:—
| Therefore the moon, the governess of floods,
| Pale in her anger, washes all the air,
| That rheumatic diseases do abound:
| And thorough this distemperature we see
| The seasons alter: hoary-headed frosts
| Fall in the fresh lap of the crimson rose;
| And on old Hyems' chin, and icy crown,
| An odorous chaplet of sweet summer buds
| Is, as in mockery, set: The spring, the summer,
| The chiding autumn, angry winter, change
| Their wonted liveries; and the 'mazed world,
| By their increase, now knows not which is which:
| And this same progeny of evils comes
| From our debate, from our dissention;
| We are their parents and original.
| *Obe.* Do you amend it then; it lies in you:
| Why should Titania cross her Oberon?
| I do but beg a little changeling boy,
| To be my henchman.
| *Tita.*   Set your heart at rest,
| The fairy land buys not the child of me.
| His mother was a vot'ress of my order:
| And, in the spiced Indian air, by night,
| Full often hath she gossip'd by my side;
| And sat with me on Neptune's yellow sands,
| Marking the embarked traders on the flood;
| When we have laugh'd to see the sails conceive,
| And grow big-bellied, with the wanton wind:
| Which she, with pretty and with swimming gait,
| (Following her womb, then rich with my young 'squire,)
| Would imitate; and sail upon the land,
| To fetch me trifles, and return again,
As from a voyage, rich with merchandise. |
But she, being mortal, of that boy did die; |
And, for her sake, do I rear up her boy: |
And, for her sake, I will not part with him. |
    Obe. How long within this wood intend you stay? |

II. 1. 139.   *Tita.* Perchance, till after Theseus' wedding-day.
If you will patiently dance in our round,
And see our moonlight revels, go with us;
If not, shun me, and I will spare your haunts.
     Obe. Give me that boy, and I will go with thee.
     Tita. Not for thy kingdom.—Fairies, away:
We shall chide down-right, if I longer stay.
                [*Exeunt* TITANIA *and her Train.*
     Obe. Well, go thy way: thou shalt not from this grove,
Till I torment thee for this injury.—
My gentle Puck, come hither: Thou remember'st
Since once I sat upon a promontory,
And heard a mermaid, on a dolphin's back,
Uttering such dulcet and harmonious breath,
That the rude sea grew civil at her song;
And certain stars shot madly from their spheres,
To hear the sea-maid's music.
     Puck.   I remember.
     Obe. That very time I saw, (but thou couldst not,)
Flying between the cold moon and the earth,
Cupid all arm'd: a certain aim he took
At a fair vestal, throned by the west;
And loos'd his love-shaft smartly from his bow,
As it should pierce a hundred thousand hearts:
But I might see young Cupid's fiery shaft
Quench'd in the chaste beams of the wat'ry moon;
And the imperial vot'ress passed on,
In maiden meditation, fancy-free.
Yet mark'd I where the bolt of Cupid fell:
It fell upon a little western flower,—
Before, milk-white; now purple with love's wound,—
And maidens call it, love-in-idleness.
Fetch me that flower; the herb I show'd thee once;
The juice of it on sleeping eyelids laid,
Will make or man or woman madly dote
| Upon the next live creature that it sees.
| Fetch me this herb: and be thou here again,
| Ere the leviathan can swim a league.
| *Puck.* I 'll put a girdle round about the earth
| In forty minutes.   [*Exit* PUCK.

II. i. 176. | *Obe.*   Having once this juice,
| I 'll watch Titania when she is asleep,
| And drop the liquor of it in her eyes:
| The next thing then she waking looks upon,
| (Be it on lion, bear, or wolf, or bull,
| On meddling monkey, or on busy ape,)
| She shall pursue it with the soul of love.
| And ere I take this charm off from her sight,
| (As I can take it, with another herb,)
| I 'll make her render up her page to me.
| But who comes here? I am invisible;
| And I will overhear their conference.

II. i. 249.   *Obe.* I know a bank whereon the wild thyme blows,
Where ox-lips and the nodding violet grows;
Quite over-canopied with lush woodbine,
With sweet musk-roses, and with eglantine:
There sleeps Titania, some time of the night,
Lull'd in these flowers with dances and delight;
And there the snake throws her enamell'd skin,
Weed wide enough to wrap a fairy in:

SCENE III—*Another Part of the Wood*

Enter TITANIA, *with her Train*

II. ii. 1. | *Tita.* Come, now a roundel and a fairy song;
| Then, for the third part of a minute, hence;
| Some, to kill cankers in the musk-rose buds;
| Some, war with rear-mice for their leathern wings,
| To make my small elves coats; and some, keep back
| The clamorous owl, that nightly hoots, and wonders
| At our quaint spirits: sing me now asleep;
| Then to your offices, and let me rest.

SONG

| *1 Fai.* You spotted snakes, with double tongue,
| Thorny hedge-hogs, be not seen;
| Newts, and blind worms, do no wrong;
| Come not near our fairy queen:

Chorus.   Philomel, with melody,
                Sing in our sweet lullaby;
Lulla, lulla, lullaby; lulla, lulla, lullaby:
                Never harm, nor spell nor charm,
                Come our lovely lady nigh;
                So, good night, with lullaby.

2 Fai. Weaving spiders, come not here;
                Hence, you long-legg'd spinners, hence:
Beetles black, approach not near;
                Worm, nor snail, do no offence.

Chorus.   Philomel, with melody, &c.

1 Fai. Hence, away; now all is well:
                One, aloof, stand sentinel.
                              [*Exeunt Fairies.* TITANIA *sleeps.*

Enter OBERON

Obe. What thou seest when thou dost wake,
                [*Squeezes the Flower on* TITANIA'S *Eyelids.*
                Do it for thy true love take;
                Love, and languish for his sake:
                Be it ounce, or cat, or bear,
                Pard, or boar with bristled hair,
                In thy eye that shall appear
                When thou wak'st, it is thy dear;
                Wake, when some vile thing is near.   [*Exit.*

Enter LYSANDER *and* HERMIA

Lys. Fair love, you faint with wandering in the wood;
And, to speak truth, I have forgot our way;
We 'll rest us, Hermia, if you think it good,
And tarry for the comfort of the day.
   Her. Be it so, Lysander: find you out a bed,
For I upon this bank will rest my head.
   Lys. One turf shall serve as pillow for us both;
One heart, one bed, two bosoms, and one troth.

II. ii. 53. | *Her.* Lysander riddles very prettily:—

II. ii. 76.   *Puck.* Pretty soul!

II. ii. 99.   *Hel.* Made me compare with Hermia's sphery eyne?

ACT III

Scene I—*The same. The Queen of Fairies lying asleep*

Re-enter Puck, *and* Bottom *with an* Ass's *Head*

III. i. 112. | *Puck.* I 'll follow you, I 'll lead you about a round,
| Through bog, through bush, through brake, through brier;
| Sometime a horse I 'll be, sometime a hound,
| A hog, a headless bear, sometime a fire;
| And neigh, and bark, and grunt, and roar, and burn,
| Like horse, hound, hog, bear, fire, at every turn.

III. i. 131.   *Bot.*   The ousel-cock, so black of hue,
                  With orange-tawney bill,
           The throstle with his note so true,
              The wren with little quill;

    Tita. What angel wakes me from my flowery bed?

                                      [Waking.

      Bot.   The finch, the sparrow, and the lark,
              The plain song cuckoo gray,
          Whose note full many à man doth mark,
            And dares not answer, nay;—

III. i. 159. | *Tita.* Out of this wood do not desire to go;
| Thou shalt remain here, whether thou wilt or no.
| I am a spirit, of no common rate;
| The summer still doth tend upon my state,
| And I do love thee: therefore, go with me;
| I 'll give thee fairies to attend on thee;
| And they shall fetch thee jewels from the deep:
| And sing, while thou on pressed flowers dost sleep:
| And I will purge thy mortal grossness so,
| That thou shalt like an airy spirit go.—
| Peas-blossom! Cobweb! Moth! and Mustard-seed!

Enter four Fairies

III. i. 171.   *Tita.* Be kind and courteous to this gentleman; |
     Hop in his walks, and gambol in his eyes; |
     Feed him with apricocks and dewberries, |
     With purple grapes, green figs, and mulberries; |
     The honey bags steal from the humble-bees, |

III. i. 176.   And, for night tapers, crop their waxen thighs,
And light them at the fiery glow-worm's eyes,
To have my love to bed, and to arise;
And pluck the wings from painted butterflies,
To fan the moon-beams from his sleeping eyes:
Nod to him, elves, and do him courtesies.

1. *Fai.* Hail, mortal!

2. *Fai.* Hail!

3. *Fai.* Hail!

4. *Fai.* Hail!

Bot. I cry your worship's mercy, heartily.—I beseech, your worship's name.

Cob. Cobweb.

Bot. I shall desire you of more acquaintance, good master Cobweb: if I cut my finger, I shall make bold with you. Your name, honest gentleman?

Peas. Peas-blossom.

Bot. I pray you, commend me to mistress Squash, your mother, and to master Peascod, your father. Good master Peas-blossom, I shall desire you of more acquaintance too.—Your name, I beseech you, sir?

Mus. Mustard-seed.

Bot. Good master Mustard-seed, I know your patience well: that same cowardly, giant-like ox-beef hath devoured many a gentleman of your house: I promise you, your kindred hath made my eyes water ere now. I desire your more acquaintance, good master Mustard-seed.

Tita. Come, wait upon him; lead him to my bower.
The moon, methinks, looks with a watery eye;
And when she weeps, weeps every little flower,
Lamenting some enforced chastity.
Tie up my love's tongue, bring him silently.   [*Exeunt.*

SCENE II—*Another Part of the Wood*

III. ii. 19.   *Puck.*   when they him spy,
As wild geese that the creeping fowler eye,
Or russet-pated choughs, many in sort,
Rising and cawing at the gun's report
Sever themselves, and madly sweep the sky;
So, at his sight, away his fellows fly:

III. ii. 60.   *Dem.* Yet you, the murderer, look as bright, as clear,
As yonder Venus in her <u>glimmering sphere.</u>

III. ii. 94.   *Obe.* About the wood go <u>swifter than the wind,</u>

III. ii. 114. | *Puck.* Shall we their fond pageant see?
| Lord, what fools these mortals be!

III. ii. 124.   *Lys.* Look, when I vow, I weep; and vows so born,
| In their nativity all truth appears.

III. ii. 141.   *Dem.* That pure congealed white, <u>high Taurus' snow,</u>
<u>Fann'd with the eastern wind,</u> turns to a crow,
When thou hold'st up thy hand:

III. ii. 177.   *Her.* Dark night, that from the eye his function takes, |
The ear more quick of apprehension makes; |

III. ii. 187.   *Lys.* Fair Helena; who more engilds the night
Than all yon fiery oes and eyes of light. |
Why seek'st thou me? could not this make thee know, |
The hate I bare thee made me leave thee so? |

III. ii. 198.   *Hel.* Is all the counsel that we two have shar'd,
The sisters' vows, the hours that we have spent,
When we have chid the <u>hasty-footed time</u>
For parting us,—O, and <u>is all forgot?</u>
All school-days' friendship, childhood innocence?
| <u>We, Hermia, like two artificial gods,</u>
| <u>Have with our neelds created both one flower,</u>
| <u>Both on one sampler, sitting on one cushion,</u>
| <u>Both warbling of one song, both in one key;</u>
| <u>As if our hands, our sides, voices, and minds,</u>
| <u>Had been incorporate. So we grew together,</u>
| <u>Like to a double cherry, seeming parted;</u>
| <u>But yet a union in partition,</u>
| <u>Two lovely berries moulded on one stem:</u>

III. ii. 232.   *Hel.* What though I be not so in grace as you,
<u>So hung upon with love,</u> so fortunate;
But miserable most, to love unlov'd?
This you should pity, rather than despise.

III. ii. 236.   *Her.* I understand not what you mean by this.
        Hel. Ay, do persevere, counterfeit sad looks,
Make mows upon me when I turn my back;
Wink at each other; hold the sweet jest up;
This sport, well carried, shall be chronicled.
If you have any pity, grace, or manners,
You would not make me such an argument.
But, fare ye well: 'tis partly my own fault;
Which death, or absence, soon shall remedy.
        Lys. Stay, gentle Helena; hear my excuse;

III. ii. 323.   *Hel.* O, when she 's angry, she is keen and shrewd:
She was a vixen, when she went to school;
And, though she be but little, she is fierce.
        Her. Little again? nothing but low and little!—
Why will you suffer her to flout me thus?
Let me come to her.
        Lys.   Get you gone, you dwarf;
You minimus, of hind'ring knot-grass made;
You bead, you acorn.

III. ii. 356. | *Obe.* The starry welkin cover thou anon
     | With drooping fog, as black as Acheron:

.   .   .   .

III. ii. 365.   With leaden legs and batty wings doth creep:

.   .   .   .   .   .

III. ii. 369.   And make his eyeballs roll with wonted sight.

III. ii. 378.   *Puck.* My fairy lord, this must be done with haste;
For night's swift dragons cut the clouds full fast,
And yonder shines Aurora's harbinger;

III. ii. 389.   *Obe.* I with the Morning's Love have oft made sport;
And, like a forester, the groves may tread,
  * Even t̄o the eastern gate, all fiery red,
Opening on Neptune with fair blessed beams,
Turns into yellow gold his salt-green streams.

     KEATS'S NOTE] * shou'd it not be—till the eastern

III. ii. 411. | *Dem.*   Yea; art thou there?
| *Puck.* Follow my voice; we 'll try no manhood here. [*Exeunt.*

| *Re-enter* LYSANDER

| *Lys.* He goes before me, and still dares me on;
| When I come where he calls, then he is gone.
| The villain is much lighter heel'd than I:
| I follow'd fast, but faster he did fly;
| That fallen am I in dark uneven way,
| And here will rest me. Come, thou gentle day!   [*Lies down.*
| For if but once thou show me thy gray light,
| I 'll find Demetrius, and revenge this spite.   [*Sleeps.*

| *Re-enter* PUCK *and* DEMETRIUS

| *Puck.* Ho, ho! ho, ho! Coward, why com'st thou not?
| *Dem.* Abide me, if you dar'st; for well I wot,
| Thou runn'st before me, shifting every place;
| And dar'st not stand, nor look me in the face.
| Where art thou?
| *Puck.*   Come hither; I am here.
| *Dem.* Nay, then thou mock'st me. Thou shalt buy this dear,
| If ever I thy face by daylight see:
| Now, go thy way. Faintness constraineth me
| To measure out my length on this cold bed.—
| By day's approach look to be visited.   [*Lies down and sleeps.*

ACT IV

SCENE I—*The same*

IV. i. 1. | *Tita.* Come, sit thee down upon this flowery bed,
| While I thy amiable cheeks do coy,
| And stick musk-roses in thy sleek smooth head,
| And kiss thy fair large ears, my gentle joy.
| *Bot.* Where 's Peas-blossom?
| *Peas.* Ready.
| *Bot.* Scratch my head, Peas-blossom.—Where 's monsieur
| Cobweb?
| *Cob.* Ready.
| *Bot.* Monsieur Cobweb; good monsieur, get your weapons
| in your hand, and kill me a red-hipped humble-bee on the top of

a thistle; and, good monsieur, bring me the honey-bag. Do not
fret yourself too much in the action, monsieur; and, good monsieur, have a care the honey-bag break not; I would be loath to
have you overflown with a honey-bag, signior.—Where 's monsieur Mustardseed?

Mus. Ready.

Bot. Give me your neif, monsieur Mustardseed. Pray you,
leave your courtesy, good monsieur.

Mus. What 's your will?

Bot. Nothing, good monsieur, but to help cavalero Cobweb
to scratch. I must to the barber's, monsieur; for methinks, I am
marvellous hairy about the face: and I am such a tender ass, if
my hair do but tickle me, I must scratch.

Tita. What, wilt thou hear some music, my sweet love?

Bot. I have a reasonable good ear in music: let us have the
tongs and the bones.

Tita. Or say, sweet love, what thou desir'st to eat.

Bot. Truly, a peck of provender; I could munch your good dry
oats. Methinks, I have a great desire to a bottle of hay: good hay,
sweet hay, hath no fellow.

Tita. I have a venturous fairy that shall seek
The squirrel's hoard, and fetch thee new nuts.

IV. i. 48.   *Tita.* So doth the woodbine, the sweet honeysuckle,
Gently entwist,—the female ivy so
Enrings the barky fingers of the elm.

V. i. 59.   *Obe.* And that same dew which sometime on the buds
Was wont to swell, like round and orient pearls,
Stood now within the pretty flowrets' eyes,
Like tears, that did their own disgrace bewail.

                    .   .   .   .

IV. i. 74.   And think no more of this night's accidents,
But as the fierce vexation of a dream.
But first I will release the fairy queen.
            Be, as thou wast wont to be;
                            [*Touching her Eyes with an Herb.*
            See, as thou wast wont to see:
            Dian's bud o'er Cupid's flower
            Hath such force and blessed power.

| Now, my Titania; wake you, my sweet queen.
| *Tita.* My Oberon! What visions have I seen!
| Methought, I was enamour'd of an ass.
| *Obe.* There lies your love.
| *Tita.*   How came these things to pass?
| O, how mine eyes do loathe his visage now!
| *Obe.* Silence, a while.—Robin, take off this head.—
| Titania, music call; and strike more dead
| Than common sleep, of all these five the sense.
| *Tita.* Music, ho! music; such as charmeth sleep.
| *Puck.* Now, when thou wak'st, with thine own fool's eyes peep.
| *Obe.* Sound, music. [*Still Music.*] Come, my queen, take
| hands with me,
| And rock the ground whereon these sleepers be.
| Now thou and I are new in amity;
| And will, to-morrow midnight, solemnly,
| Dance in duke Theseus' house triumphantly,
| And bless it to all fair prosperity:
| There shall the pairs of faithful lovers be
  Wedded, with Theseus, all in jollity.

    Puck. Fairy king, attend and mark; |
        I do hear the morning lark. |
    Obe. Then, my queen, in silence sad, |
        Trip we after the night's shade: |
        We the globe can compass soon, |
        Swifter than the wand'ring moon. |
    Tita. Come, my lord: and in our flight, |
        Tell me how it came this night, |
        That I sleeping here was found, |
        With these mortals, on the ground.   [*Exeunt.* |
                      [*Horns sound within.*

    Enter THESEUS, HIPPOLYTA, EGEUS, *and Train*
    The. Go, one of you, find out the forester;—
For now our observation is perform'd:
And since we have the vaward of the day,
My love shall hear the music of my hounds.—
Uncouple in the western valley; go:
Despatch, I say, and find the forester.
We will, fair queen, up to the mountain's top,

And mark the musical confusion
Of hounds and echo in conjunction.

    Hip. I was with Hercules and Cadmus, once,
When in a wood of Crete they bay'd the bear
With hounds of Sparta: never did I hear
Such gallant chiding; for, besides the groves,
The skies, the fountains, every region near
Seem'd all one mutual cry: I never heard
So musical a discord, such sweet thunder.

    The. My hounds are bred out of the Spartan kind,
So flew'd, so sanded; and their heads are hung
With ears that sweep away the morning dew;
Crook-knee'd, and dew-lapp'd like Thessalian bulls;
Slow in pursuit, but match'd in mouth like bells,
Each under each. A cry more tunable
Was never holla'd to, nor cheer'd with horn,
In Crete, in Sparta, nor in Thessaly:

IV. i. 193.   *Dem.* These things seem small, and undistinguishable.
Like far-off mountains turned into clouds.

ACT V

SCENE I—*The Same. An Apartment in the Palace of* THESEUS

V. i. 4.   *The.* Lovers, and madmen, have such seething brains,
Such shaping fantasies, that apprehend
More than cool reason ever comprehends.
The lunatic, the lover, and the poet,
Are of imagination all compact:
One sees more devils than vast hell can hold;
That is, the madman: the lover all as frantic,
Sees Helen's beauty in a brow of Egypt:
The poet's eye, in a fine frenzy rolling,
Doth glance from heaven to earth, from earth to heaven;
And, as imagination bodies forth
The forms of things unknown, the poet's pen
Turns them to shapes, and gives to airy nothing
A local habitation, and a name.
Such tricks hath strong imagination;

V. i. 66.   *Phil.* And tragical, my noble lord, it is;
             For Pyramus therein doth kill himself.
             Which, when I saw rehears'd, I must confess,
             | Made mine eyes water; but more merry tears
             | The passion of loud laughter never shed.
                 The. What are they, that do play it?
                 Phil. Hard-handed men, that work in Athens here,
             Which never labour'd in their minds till now;
             And now have toil'd their unbreath'd memories
             With this same play, against your nuptial.

V. i. 85.   *Hip.* I love not to see wretchedness o'ercharged, |
             And duty in his service perishing. |

V. i. 93.   *The.* Where I have come, great clerks have purpos'd
             To greet me with premeditated welcomes;
             Where I have seen them shiver and look pale,
             Make periods in the midst of sentences,
             Throttle their practis'd accents in their fears,
             And, in conclusion, dumbly have broke off,
             Not paying me a welcome: . . . . .

V. i. 104.   Love, therefore, and tongue-tied simplicity,
             In least, speak most, to my capacity.

V. i. 126. | *The.* His speech was like a tangled chain; nothing impaired,
             | but all disordered. Who is next?

V. i. 372.   *The.* The iron tongue of midnight hath told twelve:
             Lovers, to bed; 'tis almost fairy time.

SCENE II

V. ii. 13.   *Puck.* And we fairies, that do run
                 By the triple Hecat's team,
             From the presence of the sun,
                 Following darkness like a dream,
             Now are frolic; not a mouse
             Shall disturb this hallow'd house:
             I am sent with broom before,
             To sweep the dust behind the door.

Enter OBERON *and* TITANIA *with their Train*

Obe.   Through this house give glimmering light,
            By the dead and drowsy fire:
        Every elf, and fairy sprite,
            Hop as light as bird from brier;
        And this ditty, after me,
        Sing and dance it trippingly.
Tita.   First rehearse this song by rote:
        To each word a warbling note,
        Hand in hand, with fairy grace,
        Will we sing, and bless this place.

               SONG AND DANCE

Obe.   Now, until the break of day,
        Through this house each fairy stray.
        To the best bride-bed will we,
        Which by us shall blessed be;
        And the issue, there create
        Ever shall be fortunate.
        So shall all the couples three
        Ever true in loving be:
        And the blots of nature's hand
        Shall not in their issue stand;
        Never mole, hare lip, nor scar,
        Nor mark prodigious, such as are
        Despised in nativity,
        Shall upon their children be.—
        With this field-dew consecrate,
        Every fairy take his gait;
        And each several chamber bless,
        Through this palace, with sweet peace:
        E'er shall it in safety rest,
        And the owner of it blest.

MEASURE FOR MEASURE

ACT I

Scene I—*An Apartment in the* Duke's *Palace*

Enter Duke, Escalus, *Lords, and Attendants*

I. i. 17.   *Duke.* For you must know, we have with special soul
Elected him.

Enter Angelo

I. i. 26.   *Duke.*   Angelo,
There is a kind of character in thy life,
That, to the observer, doth thy history
Fully unfold: thyself and thy belongings
Are not thine own so proper, as to waste
Thyself upon thy virtues, them on thee.
Heaven doth with us, as we with torches do;
Not light them for themselves: for if our virtues
Did not go forth of us, 'twere all alike
As if we had them not. Spirits are not finely touch'd,
But to fine issues: nor nature never lends
The smallest scruple of her excellence,
But, like a thrifty goddess, she determines
Herself the glory of a creditor,
Both thanks and use.

I. i. 48.   *Ang.* Let there be some more test made of my metal,
Before so noble and so great a figure
Be stamp'd upon it.

I. i. 67.   *Duke.*   I love the people,
But do not like to stage me to their eyes:

Scene II—*A Street*

Enter Lucio *and two Gentlemen*

I. ii. 63.   1 *Gent.* Which of your hips has the most profound sciatica?

SCENE III—*The same*

Enter PROVOST, CLAUDIO, JULIET, *and Officers*

I. ii. 135.   *Claud.* As surfeit is the father of much fast,
So every scope by the immoderate use
Turns to restraint: our natures do pursue
(Like rats that ravin down their proper bane,)
A thirsty evil; and when we drink, we die.

I. ii. 142.   *Lucio.* I had as lief have the foppery of freedom, as the
morality of imprisonment.—

I. ii. 157.   *Claud.* You know the lady; she is fast my wife,

. . . .

I. ii. 164.   The stealth of our most mutual entertainment,
With character too gross, is writ on Juliet.

I. ii. 167. | *Claud.* And the new deputy now for the duke,—
| Whether it be the fault and glimpse of newness;
| Or whether that the body public be
| A horse whereon the governor doth ride,
| Who, newly in the seat, that it may know
| He can command, lets it straight feel the spur:
| Whether the tyranny be in his place,
| Or in his eminence that fills it up,
| I stagger in:—But this new governor
Awakes me all the enrolled penalties,
Which have, like unscour'd armour, hung by the wall
So long, that nineteen zodiacs have gone round,
And none of them been worn; and, for a name,
Now puts the drowsy and neglected act
Freshly on me.

I. ii. 182.   *Lucio.* and thy head stands so tickle on thy shoulders, that
a milk-maid, if she be in love, may sigh it off.

I. ii. 193.   *Claud.*   for in her youth
There is a prone and speechless dialect,
Such as moves men; beside, she hath prosperous art
When she will play with reason and discourse.

SCENE IV—*A Monastery*

Enter DUKE *and* FRIAR THOMAS

I. iii. 1. | *Duke.* No; holy father; throw away that thought;
| Believe not that the dribbling dart of love
| Can pierce a complete bosom: why I desire thee
| To give me secret harbour, hath a purpose
| More grave and wrinkled than the aims and ends
| Of burning youth.

I. iii. 9.   *Duke.*   to haunt assemblies
Where youth, and cost, and witless bravery keeps.

I. iii. 19.   *Duke.* We have strict statutes, and most biting laws,
(The needful bits and curbs for headstrong steeds,)
Which for these fourteen years we have let sleep;
Even like an overgrown lion in a cave,
That goes not out to prey: now, as fond fathers
Having bound up the threat'ning twigs of birch,
Only to stick it in their children's sight,
For terror, not to use; in time the rod
Becomes more mock'd, than fear'd: so our decrees,
Dead to infliction, to themselves are dead;
| And liberty plucks justice by the nose;
The baby beats the nurse, and quite athwart
Goes all decorum.

SCENE V—*A Nunnery*

I. iv. 16.   *Lucio.* Hail, virgin, if you be; as those cheek-roses
Proclaim you are no less!

I. iv. 31.   *Lucio.* I would not—though 'tis my familiar sin
With maids to seem the lapwing, and to jest,
Tongue far from heart,—play with all virgins so:
I hold you as a thing ensky'd, and sainted;

I. iv. 41.   *Lucio.* As those that feed grow full; as blossoming time,
That from the seedness the bare fallow brings
To teeming foison; even so her plenteous womb
Expresseth his full tilth and husbandry.

Isab. Some one with child by him? <u>My cousin Juliet?</u>
Lucio. Is she your cousin?
Isab. Adoptedly; as <u>school-maids change their names,</u>
<u>By vain though apt affection.</u>

I. iv. 57.   *Lucio.* . . . lord Angelo; <u>a man, whose blood</u>
<u>Is very snow-broth;</u> one who <u>never feels</u>
<u>The wanton stings and motions of the sense;</u>
<u>But doth rebate and blunt his natural edge</u>
<u>With profits of the mind, study and fast.</u>
He (to give fear to use and liberty,
<u>Which have, for long, run by the hideous law,</u>
<u>As mice by lions,)</u> hath pick'd out an act,
<u>Under whose heavy sense</u> your brother's life
Falls into forfeit: . . . . .

I. iv. 70.   . . . . and that's <u>my pith</u>
Of business 'twixt you and your <u>poor brother.</u>

I. iv. 77.   *Lucio.*   <u>Our doubts are traitors,</u>
<u>And make us lose the good we oft might win,</u>
<u>By fearing to attempt:</u> go to lord Angelo,
And let him learn to know, <u>when maidens sue,</u>
<u>Men give like gods; but when they weep and kneel,</u>
<u>All their petitions are as freely theirs</u>
<u>As they themselves would owe them.</u>

ACT II

Scene I—*A Hall in* Angelo's *House*

II. i. 1.   *Ang.* We must not make a <u>scare-crow</u> of the law,
Setting it up to <u>fear the birds of prey,</u>
And let it keep one shape, <u>till custom make it</u>
<u>Their perch, and not their terror.</u>

II. i. 102. | *Clo.* No, indeed, sir, not of a pin; you are therein in the right:
| but, to the point: as I say, this mistress Elbow, being, as I say,
| with child, and being great belly'd, and longing, as I said, for
| prunes; and having but two in the dish, as I said, master Froth
| here, this very man, having eaten the rest, as I said, and, as I say,

| paying for them very honestly;—for, as you know, master Froth,
| I could not give you three-pence again.

    | *Froth.* No, indeed.

    | *Clo.* Very well: your being then, if you be remember'd,
| cracking the stones of the foresaid prunes.

    | *Froth.* Ay, so I did, indeed.

    | *Clo.* Why, very well: I telling you then, if you be remember'd,
| that such a one, and such a one, were past cure of the thing you
| wot of, unless they kept very good diet, as I told you,

II. i. 204.   *Elb.* thou seest, thou wicked varlet now, what's come upon
thee; thou art to continue now, thou varlet;

Scene II

II. ii. 4.   *Prov.* He hath but as offended in a dream!

II. ii. 15.   *Prov.* What shall be done, sir, with the groaning Juliet?

II. ii. 84.   *Isab.*   Even for our kitchens
We kill the fowl of season; shall we serve heaven
With less respect than we do minister
To our gross selves?

II. ii. 107.   *Isab.*   O, it is excellent
To have a giant's strength: but it is tyrannous
To use it like a giant.
    Lucio. That's well said.
    Isab. Could great men thunder
As Jove himself does, Jove would ne'er be quiet,
For every pelting, petty officer,
Would use his heaven for thunder; nothing but thunder.—
Merciful heaven!
Thou rather, with thy sharp and sulphurous bolt,
Split'st the unwedgable and gnarled oak,
Than the soft myrtle:—O, but man, proud man!
Drest in a little brief authority;
Most ignorant of what he's most assur'd,
His glassy essence,—like an angry ape,
Plays such fantastic tricks before high heaven,
As make the angels weep:

II. ii. 127.   *Isab.* Great men may jest with saints: 'tis wit in them;
But, in less, foul profanation.

II. ii. 130.   *Isab.* That in the captain's but a choleric word,
Which in the soldier is flat blasphemy.

II. ii. 134.   *Isab.* Because authority, though it err like others,
Hath yet a kind of medicine in itself,
That skins the vice o' the top: Go to your bosom;
Knock there; and ask your heart, what it doth know
That's like my brother's fault: if it confess
A natural guiltiness, such as is his,
Let it not sound a thought upon your tongue
Against my brother's life.
    Ang. She speaks, and 'tis
Such sense, that my sense breeds with it.

II. ii. 149.   *Isab.* Not with fond shekels of the tested gold,
Or stones, whose rates are either rich or poor,
As fancy values them: but with true prayers,
That shall be up in heaven, and enter there,
Ere sun-rise; prayers from preserved souls,

II. ii. 165.   *Ang.*   but it is I
That lying by the violet, in the sun,
Do, as the carrion does, not as the flower,
Corrupt with virtuous season. Can it be,
That modesty may more betray our sense
Than woman's lightness? Having waste ground enough,
Shall we desire to raze the sanctuary,
And pitch our evils there? . . . .

II. ii. 181.   . . . . Most dangerous
Is that temptation that, doth goad us on
To sin in loving virtue: never could the strumpet,
With all her double vigour, art, and nature,
Once stir my temper; but this virtuous maid
Subdues me quite;—

SCENE III

II. iii. 4.   *Duke.* I come to visit the afflicted spirits
                Here in the prison.

II. iii. 20.   *Jul.* I do; and bear the shame most patiently.

SCENE IV

II. iv. 2.   *Ang.*   heaven hath my empty words;
                Whilst my invention, hearing not my tongue,
                Anchors on Isabel: Heaven in my mouth,
                As if I did but only chew his name;
                And in my heart, the strong and swelling evil
                Of my conception: . . . . . .

II. iv. 9.   . . . . yea, my gravity,
                Wherein (let no man hear me) I take pride,
                Could I, with boot, change for an idle plume,
                Which the air beats for vain. O place; O form!
                How often dost thou with thy case, thy habit,
                Wrench awe from fools, and tie the wiser souls
                To thy false seeming?

II. iv. 25.   *Ang.* So play the foolish throngs with one that swoons;
                Come all to help him, and so stop the air
                By which he should revive:

II. iv. 41.   *Isab.*   he may be so fitted,
                That his soul sicken not.

II. iv. 46.   *Ang.*   saucy sweetness,

II. iv. 70.   *Isab.*   if it be sin,
                Heaven, let me bear it! you granting of my suit,
                If that be sin, I'll make it my morn prayer

II. iv. 113.   *Isab.*   lawful mercy is
                Nothing akin to foul redemption.

II. iv. 159.   *Ang.* That you shall stifle in your own report,
                And smell of calumny.

ACT III

Scene I

III. i. 5.   *Duke.* Be absolute for death; either death or life,
Shall thereby be the sweeter. Reason thus with life,—
If I do lose thee, I do lose a thing
That none but fools would keep: a breath thóu art,
(Servile to all the skiey influences,)
That dost this habitation, where thou keep'st,
Hourly afflict: merely, thou art death's fool;
For him thou labour'st by thy flight to shun,
And yet run'st toward him still: Thou art not noble;
For all the accommodations that thou bear'st
Are nurs'd by baseness: Thou art by no means valiant:
For thou dost fear the soft and tender fork
Of a poor worm: Thy best of rest is sleep,
And that thou oft provok'st; yet grossly fear'st
Thy death, which is no more. Thou art not thyself;
For thou exist'st on many a thousand grains
That issue out of dust: Happy thou art not:
For what thou hast not, still thou striv'st to get;
And what thou hast, forget'st; Thou art not certain;
For thy complexion shifts to strange effects,
After the moon: If thou art rich, thou art poor;
For, like an ass, whose back with ingots bows,
Thou bear'st thy heavy riches but a journey,
And death unloads thee: Friend hast thou none;
For thine own bowels, which do call thee sire,
The mere effusion of thy proper loins,
Do curse the gout, serpigo, and the rheum,
For ending thee no sooner: Thou hast nor youth, nor age;
But, as it were, an after-dinner's sleep,
Dreaming on both: for all thy blessed youth
Becomes as aged, and doth beg the alms
Of palsied eld; and when thou art old, and rich,
Thou hast neither heat, affection, limb, nor beauty,
To make thy riches pleasant. What's yet in this,
That bears the name of life? Yet in this life
Lie hid more thousand deaths: yet death we fear,
That makes these odds all even.

III. i. 55.   *Isab.* Lord Angelo, having affairs to heaven,
Intends you for his swift embassador,
Where you shall be an everlasting leiger:
Therefore your best appointment make with speed;
To-morrow you set on.

III. i. 63.   *Isab.* There is a devilish mercy in the judge,

III. i. 67.   *Isab.* Though all the world's vastidity you had,
To a determin'd scope.

III. i. 70.   *Isab.* Would bark your honour from that trunk you bear,
And leave you naked.

III. i. 72.   *Isab.* O, I do fear thee, Claudio; and I quake
Lest thou a feverous life shouldst entertain,
And six or seven winters more respect
Than a perpetual honour. Dar'st thou die?
The sense of death is most in apprehension;
And the poor beetle, that we tread upon,
In corporal sufferance finds a pang as great
As when a giant dies.

III. i. 81.   *Claud.*   If I must die,
I will encounter darkness as a bride,
And hug it in mine arms.
        Isab. There spake my brother; there my father's grave
Did utter forth a voice! Yes, thou must die:
Thou art too noble to conserve a life
In base appliances. This outward-sainted deputy,
Whose settled visage and deliberate word
Nips youth i' the head, and follies doth emmew,
As falcon doth the fowl,—is yet a devil;
His filth within being cast, he would appear
A pond as deep as hell.
        Claud.   The princely Angelo?
        Isab. O, 'tis the cunning livery of hell,
The damned'st body to invest and cover
In princely guards! Dost thou think, Claudio,
If I would yield him my virginity,
Thou might'st be freed?

III. i. 107.   *Claud.* That thus can make him <u>bite the law by the nose,</u>

III. i. 116.   *Claud.* <u>Ay, but to die, and go we know not where;</u>
<u>To lie in cold obstruction, and to rot;</u>
<u>This sensible warm motion to become</u>
<u>A kneaded cold; and the delighted spirit</u>
<u>To bathe in fiery floods, or to reside</u>
<u>In thrilling regions of thick-ribbed ice;</u>
<u>To be imprison'd in the viewless winds,</u>
<u>And blown with restless violence round about</u>
<u>The pendent world; or to be worse than worst</u>
<u>Of those, that lawless and incertain thoughts</u>
<u>Imagine howling!—'tis too horrible!</u>
<u>The weariest and most loathed worldly life,</u>
<u>That age, ache, penury, and imprisonment</u>
<u>Can lay on nature, is a paradise</u>
<u>To what we fear of death.</u>

III. i. 140.   *Isab.* <u>For such a warped slip of wilderness</u>

III. i. 218.   *Isab.* I have heard of the lady, and good words went with her |
name. |

III. i. 278. | *Duke.* I will presently to Saint Luke's; there, at the moated
| grange, resides this dejected Mariana:

Scene II—*The Street before the Prison*

III. ii. 27.   *Duke.* Canst thou believe thy living is a life,
So <u>stinkingly depending?</u>

III. ii. 117.   *Lucio.* Some report, a sea-maid spawn'd him:— |
Some, that he was begot between two stock-fishes:— |

III. ii. 137. | *Lucio.* Who? not the duke? yes, your beggar of fifty;—and
| his use was, to put a ducat in her clack-dish: the duke had crotchets
| in him: he would be drunk too; that let me inform you.

III. ii. 189.   *Lucio.* sparrows must not build in his house-eaves, because |
they are lecherous. . . . . . |

III. ii. 195.   . . . The duke, I say to thee again, would eat mutton on |
Fridays. He's now past it; yet, and I say to thee, he would |

mouth with a beggar, though she smelt brown bread and garlic: |
say, that I said so. Farewell.   [*Exit.* |

III. ii. 217.   *Bawd.* his child is a year and a quarter old, come Philip and |
Jacob: I have kept it myself; and see how he goes about to abuse |
me. |

III. ii. 272.   *Escal.* I have labour'd for the poor gentleman, to the extremest |
shore of my modesty; |

III. ii. 295.   *Duke.* How may likeness, made in crimes, |
Making practice on the times, |
Draw with idle spiders' strings |
Most pond'rous and substantial things! |

ACT IV

Scene I—*A room in* Mariana's *House*

Mariana *discovered sitting; a* Boy *singing*

Song

IV. i. 1.   Take, oh take those lips away,
That so sweetly were forsworn;
And those eyes, the break of day,
Lights that do mislead the morn;

IV. i. 30.   *Isab.* He hath a garden circummur'd with brick, |
Whose western side is with a vineyard back'd; |
And to that vineyard is a planchard gate, |
That makes his opening with this bigger key: |
This other doth command a little door, |
Which from the vineyard to the garden leads;
There have I made my promise to call on him,
Upon the heavy middle of the night.

IV. i. 41.   *Isab.* With whispering and most guilty diligence,
‖In action all of precept, he did show me
‖The way twice o'er.

IV. i. 60. | *Duke.* The vaporous night approaches.

IV. i. 61. | *Duke.* O place and greatness, millions of false eyes
| Are stuck upon thee! volumes of report

| Run with these false and most contrarious quests
| Upon thy doings! thousand 'scapes of wit
| Make thee the father of their idle dream,
| And rack thee in their fancies!—Welcome! How agreed?

Scene II—*A Room in the Prison*

IV. ii. 38.   *Clo.* Painting, sir, I have heard say, is a mystery; and your |
whores, sir, being members of my occupation, using painting, |
do prove my occupation a mystery; but what mystery there |
should be in hanging, if I should be hang'd, I cannot imagine. |

IV. ii. 66.   *Prov.* Look, here's the warrant, Claudio, for thy death:
| 'Tis now dead midnight, and by eight to-morrow
Thou must be made immortal. Where's Barnadine?
    Claud. As fast lock'd up in sleep, as guiltless labour
When it lies starkly in the traveller's bones:

IV. ii. 78. | *Prov.* None, since the curfew rung.

IV. ii. 89. | *Duke.* This is a gentle provost: Seldom, when
| The steeled gaoler is the friend of men.
How now? What noise? That spirit's possess'd with haste,
That wounds the unsisting postern with these strokes.

IV. ii. 97.   *Duke.* As near the dawning, Provost, as it is, |

IV. ii. 109.   *Mes.*   it is almost day.

IV. ii. 148.   *Prov.* A man that apprehends death no more dreadfully,
but as a drunken sleep; careless, reckless, . . . insensible of
mortality, and desperately mortal.

IV. ii. 219.   *Duke.* Look, the unfolding star calls up the shepherd: . . .

IV. ii. 226.   . . . Come away; it is almost clear dawn.

Scene III—*Another Room in the Same*

IV. iii. 4. | *Clo.* First, here's young master Rash; he's in for a commodity
| of brown paper and old ginger, nine-score and seventeen pounds;
| of which he made five marks, ready money: marry, then, ginger

| was not much in request, for the old women were all dead. Then
| is there here one master Caper, at the suit of master Three-pile
the mercer, for some four suits of peach-colour'd satin, which |
now peaches him a beggar. Then have we here young Dizy, and |
young master Deep-vow, and master Copper-spur, and master |
Starve-lackey the rapier and dagger-man, and young Drop-heir |
that kill'd lusty Pudding, and master Forthright the tilter, and |
brave master Shoe-tie the great traveller, and wild Half-can that |
stabb'd Potts, and, I think, forty more; all great doers in our |
trade, and are now for the Lord's sake. |

IV. iii. 38.   *Pom.* He is coming, sir, he is coming; <u>I hear his straw rustle.</u>

IV. iii. 47.   *Bar.* You rogue, I have been drinking all night, I am not |
                fitted for 't. |

IV. iii. 95.   *Duke.*   Ere twice
                The sun hath made his <u>journal greeting to</u>
                <u>The under generation,</u>

IV. iii. 107.   *Duke.*   and from thence, |
                By cold gradation and weal-balanced form, |
                We shall proceed with Angelo. |

Scene IV—*A Room in* Angelo's *House*

IV. iv. 26.   *Ang.*   But that <u>her tender shame</u>
               <u>Will not proclaim against her maiden loss,</u>

Scene VI—*Street near the City Gate*

IV. vi. 7.   *Isab.*   for 'tis a physic,
              <u>That 's bitter to sweet end.</u>

ACT V

Scene I—*A Public Place near the City Gate*

V. i. 6.   *Duke.*   that our soul
            | Cannot but yield you forth to public thanks,
            | Forerunning more requital.

V. i. 12.   *Duke.* A <u>forted residence, 'gainst the tooth of time,</u>
            <u>And razure of oblivion:</u>

V. i. 42.   *Isab.* Is it not <u>strange, and strange?</u>

V. i. 48.   *Isab.* O prince, I conjure thee, as thou believ'st
  | There is another comfort than this world,
  | That thou neglect me not, with that opinion
  | That I am touch'd with madness: make not impossible
  | That which but seems unlike:

V. i. 59. | *Duke.*   By mine honesty,
  | If she be mad, (as I believe no other,)
  | Her madness hath the oddest frame of sense,
  | Such <u>a dependency of thing on thing,</u>
  | As e'er I heard in madness.

V. i. 115.   *Isab.*   And is this all?
  | Then, oh, you blessed ministers above,
  | Keep me in patience; and, with ripen'd time,
  | Unfold the evil which is here wrapt up
  | In countenance!—Heaven shield your grace from woe,
  | As I, thus wrong'd, hence unbelieved go!

V. i. 289.   *Duke.*   and let the devil
  | Be sometime honour'd for his burning throne:—

V. i. 316.   *Duke.* Where I have seen corruption boil and bubble, |
  Till it o'er-run the stew: laws, for all faults; |
  But faults so countenanc'd, that the strong statutes |
  Stand like the forfeits in a barber's shop, |
  As much in mock as mark. |

V. i. 351. | *Lucio.* Come, sir; come, sir; come, sir; foh, sir: Why, you
  | bald-pated, lying rascal! you must be hooded, must you? Show
  | your knave's visage, with a pox to you! show your sheep-biting
  | face, and be hang'd an hour! Will 't not off?
                             [*Pulls off the Friar's Hood.*

V. i. 370.   *Ang.* When I perceive, your grace, <u>like power divine,</u>
<u>Hath looked upon my passes:</u>

V. i. 398.   *Duke.* <u>That life is better life, past fearing death,</u>
<u>Than that which lives to fear:</u>

V. i. 436.   *Duke.* Her brother's ghost his <u>paved bed</u> would break,

ANTONY AND CLEOPATRA

ACT I

Scene I—*Alexandria. A Room in* Cleopatra's *Palace*

Enter Demetrius *and* Philo

I. i. 1.
    | *Phi.* Nay, but this dotage of our general's
    | O'erflows the measure: those his goodly eyes,
    | That o'er the files and musters of the war
    | Have glow'd like plated Mars, now bend, now turn,
    | The office and devotion of their view
    | Upon a tawny front: his captain's heart,
    | Which in the scuffles of great fights hath burst
    | The buckles on his breast, reneges all temper;
    | And is become the bellows, and the fan,
    | To cool a gipsy's lust.

I. i. 14.
    | *Cleo.* If it be love indeed, tell me how much.

I. i. 29.
    Cleo.   As I am Egypt's queen,
Thou blushest, Antony; and that blood of thine
    | Is Cæsar's homager: else so thy cheek pays shame,
When shrill-tongu'd Fulvia scolds.—

I. i. 48.
    Ant.   * Fie, wrangling queen!
Whom every thing becomes, to chide, to laugh,
To weep; whose every passion fully strives
To make itself, in thee, fair and admir'd!

Scene II—*The same. Another Room*

Enter Charmian, Iras, Alexas, *and a Soothsayer*

I. ii. 91.
    Cleo. A Roman thought hath struck him.

I. ii. 132.
    Ant. What our contempts doth often hurl from us,
We wish it ours again; the present pleasure,
By revolution lowering, does become
The opposite of itself:

KEATS'S NOTE] * How much more Shakespeare delights in dwelling upon the romantic and wildly natural than upon the monumental. see Winter's Tale, "When you do dance," &c.

I. ii. 146.   *Eno.* Under a compelling occasion, let women die: It were |
pity to cast them away for nothing; though, between them and |
a great cause, they should be esteemed nothing. Cleopatra, |
catching but the least noise of this, dies instantly; I have seen her |
die twenty times upon far poorer moment: I do think, there is |
mettle in death, which commits some loving act upon her, she |
hath such a celerity in dying. |

I. ii. 197.   *Ant.* Hath given the dare to Caesar,

I. ii. 205. | *Ant.*   Much is breeding,
| Which, like the courser's hair, hath yet but life,
| And not a serpent's poison. Say, our pleasure,
| To such whose place is under us, requires
Our quick remove from hence.

SCENE III—*The same. Another room*

Enter CLEOPATRA, CHARMIAN, IRAS, *and* ALEXAS

I. iii. 2.   *Cleo.* See where he is, who's with him, what he does:—
| I did not send you;—If you find him sad,
| Say, I am dancing; if in mirth, report
| That I am sudden sick: Quick, and return.   [*Exit* ALEX.

I. iii. 10.   *Cleo.* Thou teachest like a fool: the way to lose him.

I. iii. 13. | *Cleo.*   I am sick, and sullen.
| *Ant.* I am sorry to give breathing to my purpose,—
| *Cleo.* Help me away, dear Charmian, I shall fall;
| It cannot be thus long, the sides of nature
| Will not sustain it.
| *Ant.*   Now, my dearest queen,—
| *Cleo.* Pray you, stand farther from me.
| *Ant.*   What's the matter ?
| *Cleo.* I know, by that same eye, there's some good news.
| What says the married woman ?—You may go;
| 'Would she had never given you leave to come!
| Let her not say, 'tis I that keep you here,
| I have no power upon you; hers you are.
| *Ant.* The gods best know,—
| *Cleo.*   O, never was there queen

| So mightily betray'd! Yet, at the first,
| I saw the treasons planted.
| *Ant.*   Cleopatra,—
| *Cleo.* Why should I think, you can be mine, and true,
| Though you in swearing shake the throned gods,
| Who have been false to Fulvia? Riotous madness,
| To be entangled with those mouth-made vows,
| Which break themselves in swearing!

I. iii. 35.   *Cleo.* <u>Eternity was in our lips, and eyes;</u>

I. iii. 43.   *Ant.*   but my full heart
| Remains in use with you. Our Italy
| Shines o'er with civil swords: Sextus Pompeius
| Makes his approaches to the port of Rome:
| Equality of two domestic powers
| Breed <u>scrupulous faction</u>: The hated, grown to strength,
| Are newly grown to love:

I. iii. 59.   *Ant.* She's dead, my queen:
| Look here, and, at thy sovereign leisure, read
| The garboils she awak'd; at the last, best:
| See, when, and where she died.

I. iii. 99. | *Cleo.* And all the gods go with you! upon your sword
| Sit laurel'd victory! and smooth success
| Be strew'd before your feet!

SCENE IV—*Rome. An Apartment in* CÆSAR'S *House*
Enter OCTAVIUS CÆSAR, LEPIDUS, *and Attendants*

I. iv. 16. | *Cæs.* You are too indulgent: Let us grant, it is not
| Amiss <u>to tumble on the bed of Ptolemy</u>;
| To give a kingdom for a mirth; to sit
| And keep the turn of tippling with a slave;
| To reel the streets at noon, and stand the buffet
| With knaves that smell of sweat: say, this becomes him
| (As his composure must be rare indeed,
| Whom these things cannot blemish), yet must Antony
| No way excuse his soils, when we do bear
| So great weight in his lightness. If he fill'd

| His vacancy with his voluptuousness,
| Full surfeits, and the dryness of his bones,
| Call on him for 't:

I. iv. 30.   *Cæs.*   'tis to be chid
As we rate boys; who, being mature in knowledge,
Pawn their experience to their present pleasure,
And so rebel to judgement.

I. iv. 44.   *Cæs.*   This common body,
Like a vagabond flag upon the stream,
Goes to, and back, lackeying the varying tide,
To rot itself with motion.

I. iv. 55. | *Cæs.*   Antony,
| Leave thy lascivious wassels. When thou once
| Wast beaten from Modena, where thou slew'st
| Hirtius and Pansa, consuls, at thy heel
| Did famine follow; whom thou fought'st against,
| Though daintily brought up, with patience more
| Than savages could suffer: Thou didst drink
| The stale of horses, and the gilded puddle
| Which beasts would cough at: thy palate then did deign
| The roughest berry on the rudest hedge;
| Yea, like the stag, when snow the pasture sheets,
| The barks of trees thou browsed'st; on the Alps
| It is reported, thou didst eat strange flesh,
| Which some did die to look on: And all this
| (It wounds thine honour that I speak it now),
| Was borne so like a soldier, that thy cheek
| So much as lank'd not.

SCENE V—*Alexandria. A Room in the Palace*

Enter CLEOPATRA, CHARMIAN, IRAS, *and* MARDIAN

I. v. 18. | *Cleo.*   O Charmian,
| Where think'st thou he is now? Stands he, or sits he?
| Or does he walk? or is he on his horse?
| O happy horse, to bear the weight of Antony!
| Do bravely, horse! for wot'st thou whom thou mov'st?
| The demi-Atlas of this earth, the arm

| And burgonet of men.—He's speaking now,
| Or murmuring, *Where's my serpent of old Nile?*
| For so he calls me; Now I feed myself
| With most delicious poison:—Think on me,
| That am with Phœbus' amorous pinches black,
| And wrinkled deep in time? Broad-fronted Cæsar,
| When thou wast here above the ground, I was
| A morsel for a monarch: and great Pompey
| Would stand, and make his eyes grow in my brow;
| There would he anchor his aspéct, and die
| With looking on his life.

I. v. 42.   *Alex.*   Good friend, quoth he,
| *Say, the firm Roman to great Egypt sends*
| *This treasure of an oyster; at whose foot,*
| *To mend the petty present, I will piece*
| *Her opulent throne with kingdoms; All the east,*
| Say thou, *shall call her mistress.* So he nodded,
| And soberly did mount a termagant steed,
| Who neigh'd so high, that what I would have spoke
| Was beastly dumb'd by him.

I. v. 53. | *Cleo.* O well-divided disposition!—Note him,
| Note him, good Charmian, 'tis the man; but note him:
| He was not sad; for he would shine on those
| That make their looks by his: he was not merry;
| Which seem'd to tell them, his remembrance lay
| In Egypt with his joy: but between both:
| O heavenly mingle!—Be'st thou sad, or merry,
| The violence of either thee becomes;

I. v. 63. | *Cleo.*   Who's born that day
| When I forget to send to Antony,
| Shall die a beggar.—Ink and paper, Charmian.—
| Welcome, my good Alexas.—Did I, Charmian,
| Ever love Cæsar so?
      Char.   O that brave Cæsar!
| *Cleo.* Be chok'd with such another emphasis!
| Say, the brave Antony.
      Char.   The valiant Cæsar!

| *Cleo.* By Isis, I will give thee bloody teeth,
| If thou with Cæsar paragon again
| My man of men.
| *Char.*   By your most gracious pardon,
| I sing but after you.
| *Cleo.*   <u>My salad days;</u>
| When I was green in judgement:—Cold in blood,
| To say as I said then!—But, come, away:
| Get me ink and paper:

ACT II

SCENE I—*Messina. A Room in* POMPEY'S *House*

Enter POMPEY, MENECRATES, *and* MENAS

II. i. 1.

 Pom. If the great gods be just, they shall assist
The deeds of justest men.
 Mene.   Know, worthy Pompey,
That what they do delay, they not deny.
 Pom. Whiles we are suitors to their throne, decays
The thing we sue for.
 Mene.   We, ignorant of ourselves,
Beg often our own harms, which the wise powers
Deny us for our good; so find we profit,
By losing of our prayers.
 Pom.   I shall do well:
The people love me, and the sea is mine;
My powers are crescent, and my auguring hope
Says, it will come to the full. Mark Antony
In Egypt sits at dinner, and will make
No wars without doors: Cæsar gets money, where
He loses hearts: Lepidus flatters both,
Of both is flatter'd;

II. i. 19.

 Pom. He dreams; I know, they are in Rome together,
| Looking for Antony: But all charms of love,
| Salt Cleopatra, soften thy wan'd lip!
| Let witchcraft join with beauty, lust with both!
| Tie up the libertine in a field of feasts,
| Keep his brain fuming; Epicurean cooks,
| Sharpen with cloyless sauce his appetite;

| That sleep and feeding may prorogue his honour,
| Even till a Lethe'd dullness.—

II. i. 35.   *Pom.*   But let us rear
The higher our opinion, that our stirring
| Can from the lap of Egypt's widow pluck
| The ne'er lust-wearied Antony.

II. ii. 9.   *Eno.*   Every time
Serves for the matter that is then born in it.

II. ii. 199.   *Eno.* The barge she sat in, like a burnish'd throne,
| Burn'd on the water: the poop was beaten gold;
| Purple the sails, and so perfum'd, that
| The winds were love-sick with them: the oars were silver;
| Which to the tune of flutes kept stroke, and made
| The water, which they beat, to follow faster,
| As amorous of their strokes. For her own person,
| It beggar'd all description: she did lie
| In her pavilion (cloth of gold, of tissue),
| O'er-picturing that Venus, where we see,
| The fancy out-work nature: on each side her,
| Stood pretty dimpled boys, like smiling Cupids,
| With diverse-colour'd fans, whose wind did seem
| To glow the delicate cheeks which they did cool,
| And what they undid, did.
| *Agr.*   O, rare for Antony!
| *Eno.* Her gentlewomen, like the Nereides,
| So many mermaids, tended her i' the eyes,
| And made their bends adornings: at the helm
| A seeming mermaid steers; the silken tackle
| Swell with the touches of those flower-soft hands,
| That yarely frame the office. From the barge
| A strange invisible pérfume hits the sense
| Of the adjacent wharfs. The city cast
| Her people out upon her; and Antony,
| Enthron'd in the market-place, did sit alone,
| Whistling to the air; which, but for vacancy,
| Had gone to gaze on Cleopatra too,
| And made a gap in nature.

II. ii. 236.   *Eno.*   I saw her once
Hop forty paces through the public street:
And having lost her breath, she spoke and panted,
That she did make defect, perfection,
And, breathless, power breathe forth.
     Mec. Now Antony must leave her utterly.
     Eno. Never; he will not:
Age cannot wither her, nor custom stale
Her infinite variety: Other women
Cloy th' appetites they feed; but she makes hungry,
Where most she satisfies. For vilest things
Become themselves in her; that the holy priests
Bless her, when she is riggish.

SCENE III—*The same. A Room in* CÆSAR's *House*

Enter CÆSAR, ANTONY, OCTAVIA *between them; Attendants
and a Soothsayer*

II. iii. 13.   *Ant.* If you can, your reason?
     Sooth.   I see 't in
My motion, have it not in my tongue: But yet
Hie you again to Egypt.
     Ant.   Say to me,
Whose fortunes shall rise higher, Cæsar's or mine?
     Sooth. Cæsar's.
Therefore, O Antony, stay not by his side:
Thy dæmon, that's thy spirit which keeps thee, is
Noble, courageous, high, unmatchable,
Where Cæsar's is not; but, near him, thy angel
Becomes a fear, as being o'erpower'd; therefore
Make space enough between you.
     Ant.   Speak this no more.
     Sooth. To none but thee; no more, but when to thee.
If thou dost play with him at any game,
Thou art sure to lose; and, of that natural luck,
He beats thee 'gainst the odds; thy lustre thickens,
When he shines by: I say again, thy spirit
Is all afraid to govern thee near him;
But, he away, 'tis noble.

   Ant.   Get thee gone: [*Exit* Sooth.
Say to Ventidius, I would speak with him:
He shall to Parthia.—Be it art, or hap,
He hath spoken true: The very dice obey him;
And in our sports, my better cunning faints
Under his chance: if we draw lots, he speeds:
His cocks do win the battle still of mine,
When it is all to nought; and his quails ever
Beat mine, inhoop'd, at odds. I will to Egypt:
And though I make this marriage for my peace,

     Enter VENTIDIUS
I' the east my pleasure lies:—O, come, Ventidius,
You must to Parthia; your commission 's ready:
Follow me, and receive it.   [*Exeunt.*

   SCENE V—*Alexandria. A Room in the Palace*
   Enter CLEOPATRA, CHARMIAN, IRAS, *and* ALEXAS

II. v. 10. *Cleo.* Give me mine angle,—We'll to the river: there,
My music playing far off, I will betray
Tawny-finn'd fishes; my bended hook shall pierce
Their slimy jaws; and, as I draw them up,
I'll think them every one an Antony,
And say, Ah, ha! you're caught.
   Char.   'Twas merry, when
You wager'd on your angling; when your diver
Did hang a salt-fish on his hook, which he
With fervency drew up.
   Cleo.   That time!—O times!—
I laugh'd him out of patience; and that night
I laugh'd him into patience: and next morn,
Ere the ninth hour, I drunk him to his bed;
Then put my tires and mantles on him, whilst
I wore his sword Philippan.

II. v. 28. *Cleo.*   and here
My bluest veins to kiss; a hand, that kings
Have lipp'd, and trembled kissing.

II. v. 94. *Cleo.* So half my Egypt were submerg'd, and made
A cistern for scal'd snakes!

II. v. 111.   *Cleo.* <u>Go to the fellow, good Alexas; bid him</u>
<u>Report the feature of Octavia, her years,</u>
<u>Her inclination, let him not leave out</u>
<u>The colour of her hair:</u>

II. v. 118.   *Cleo.* <u>Bring me word, how tall she is.</u>

Scene VI—*Near Misenum*

II. vi. 17.   *Pom.*   <u>courtiers of beauteous freedom,</u>
To drench the Capitol; but that they would
Have one man but a man? And that is it,
Hath made me rig my navy; at whose burden |
The anger'd ocean foams; with which I meant |
To scourge the ingratitude that despiteful Rome |
Cast on my noble father.

II. vi. 26.   *Pom.*   At land, indeed,
Thou dost o'er-count me of my father's house: |
But, since the cuckoo builds not for himself, |
Remain in 't, as thou mayst. |

II. vi. 50. | *Ant.* The beds i' the east are soft; and thanks to you,
| That call'd me, timelier than my purpose, hither;

II. vi. 75.   *Eno.*   Sir, |
I never lov'd you much; but I have prais'd you, |
When you have well deserv'd ten times as much |
As I have said you did. |

Scene VII—*On board* Pompey's *Galley, lying near Misenum*

II. vii. 13.   *Sec. Serv.* <u>I had as lief have a reed that will do me no service,</u>
<u>as a partizan I could not heave.</u>
    First Serv. <u>To be called into a huge sphere, and not to be seen</u>
<u>to move in 't, are the holes where eyes should be, which pitifully</u>
<u>disaster the cheeks.</u>

II. vii. 20. | *Ant.* Thus do they, sir: [*To* Cæsar] They take the flow o' the
| Nile
| By certain scales i' the pyramid; they know,

| By the height, the lowness, or the mean, if dearth,
| Or foizon, follow: The higher Nilus swells,
| The more it promises: as it ebbs, the seedsman
| Upon the slime and ooze scatters his grain,
| And shortly comes to harvest.
| *Lep.* You have strange serpents there.
| *Ant.* Ay, Lepidus.
| *Lep.* Your serpent of Egypt is bred now of your mud, by the
| operation of your sun: so is your crocodile.
| *Ant.* They are so.
| *Pom.* Sit,—and some wine.—A health to Lepidus.
| *Lep.* I am not so well as I should be, but I 'll ne'er out.
| *Eno.* Not till you have slept; I fear me, you 'll be in, till then.
| *Lep.* Nay, certainly, I have heard, the Ptolemies' pyramises
| are very goodly things; without contradiction, I have heard that.
| *Men.* Pompey, a word.   [*Aside.*
| *Pom.*   Say in mine ear: What is 't?
| *Men.* Forsake thy seat, I do beseech thee, captain,
| And hear me speak a word.   [*Aside.*
| *Pom.*   Forbear me till anon.—
| This wine for Lepidus.

II. vii. 74.   *Men.* Thou art, if thou dar'st be, the earthly Jove:
‖ Whate'er the ocean pales, or sky inclips,
‖ Is thine, if thou wilt have 't.

II. vii. 114.   *Ant.* Till that the conquering wine hath steep'd our sense
In soft and delicate Lethe.
              Eno.   All take hands.—
‖ Make battery to our ears with the loud music:—
‖ The while, I 'll place you: Then the boy shall sing;
‖ The holding every man shall bear, as loud
‖ As his strong sides can volley.
              [*Music plays. Enobarbus places them Hand in Hand.*

II. vii. 130.   *Cæs.*   and mine own tongue
Splits what it speaks; the wild disguise hath almost
Antick'd us all.

II. vii. 137. | *Men.*   No, to my cabin.—
              | These drums!—these trumpets, flutes! what!—

| Let Neptune hear we bid a loud farewell
| To these great fellows: Sound, and be hang'd, sound out.

[A Flourish of Trumpets, with Drums.

ACT III

Scene I—*A plain in Syria*

III. i. 1.   *Ven.* Now, <u>darting Parthia</u>, art thou struck;

III. i. 12.   *Ven.*   A lower place, note well,
| May make too great an act: For learn this, Silius;
| Better leave undone, than by our deed acquire
| Too high a fame, when him we serve's away.
| Cæsar, and Antony, have ever won
| More in their officer, than person: Sossius,
| One of my place in Syria, his lieutenant,
| For quick accumulation of renown,
| Which he achiev'd by the minute, lost his favour.
| Who does i' the wars more than his captain can,
| Becomes his captain's captain: and ambition,
| The soldier's virtue, rather makes choice of loss,
| Than gain, which darkens him.
| I could do more to do Antonius good,
| But 'twould offend him; and in his offence
| Should my performance perish.
          Sil.   Thou hast, Ventidius,
| That without which a soldier, and his sword,
| Grants scarce distinction. Thou wilt write to Antony?
| *Ven.* I'll humbly signify what in his name,
| That magical word of war, we have effected;
| How, with his banners, and his well-paid ranks,
| The ne'er-yet-beaten horse of Parthia
| We have jaded out o' the field.

Scene II—*Rome*

III. ii. 20.   *Eno.* <u>They are his shards, and he their beetle.</u>

III. ii. 42.   *Oct.* My noble brother!—
| *Ant.* The April's in her eyes: It is love's spring,
| And these the showers to bring it on.—Be cheerful.

III. ii. 48.   *Ant.*   <u>the swan's down feather,</u>
<u>That stands upon the swell at full of tide,</u>
<u>And neither way inclines.</u>

SCENE III—*Alexandria. A Room in the Palace*

III. iii. 7.   *Mess.* Most gracious majesty,—
    Cleo.   Didst thou behold Octavia?
    Mess. Ay, dread queen.
    Cleo.   Where?
    Mess.   Madam, in Rome
I look'd her in the face; and saw her led
Between her brother and Mark Antony.
    Cleo. Is she as tall as me?
    Mess.   She is not, madam.
    Cleo. Didst hear her speak? is she shrill-tongu'd, or low?
    Mess. Madam, I heard her speak; she is low-voic'd.
    Cleo. That's not so good:—he cannot like her long.
    Char. Like her? O Isis! 'tis impossible.
    Cleo. I think so, Charmian: Dull of tongue, and dwarfish!—
What majesty is in her gait? Remember,
If e'er thou look'st on majesty.
    Mess.   She creeps;
Her motion and her station are as one:
She shows a body rather than a life;
A statue, than a breather.
    Cleo.   Is this certain?
    Mess. Or I have no observance.
    Char.   Three in Egypt
Cannot make better note.
    Cleo.   He's very knowing,
I do perceive 't:—There's nothing in her yet:—
The fellow has good judgement.
    Char.   Excellent.
    Cleo. Guess at her years, I pr'ythee.
    Mess.   Madam,
She was a widow,—
    Cleo.   Widow?—Charmian, hark.
    Mess. And I do think, she's thirty.
    Cleo. Bear'st thou her face in mind? is 't long, or round?

| *Mess.* Round even to faultiness.

| *Cleo.*   For the most part, too,
| They are foolish that are so.—Her hair, what colour?

| *Mess.* Brown, madam: And her forehead is as low
| As she would wish it.

| *Cleo.*   There is gold for thee.
| Thou must not take my former sharpness ill:—
| I will employ thee back again; I find thee
| Most fit for business: Go make thee ready;
| Our letters are prepar'd.   [*Exit* Messenger.

| *Char.*   A proper man.

| *Cleo.* Indeed, he is so: I repent me much,
| That so I harry'd him. Why, methinks, by him,
| This creature's no such thing.

| *Char.*   O, nothing, madam.

| *Cleo.* The man hath seen some majesty and should know.

| *Char.* Hath he seen majesty? Isis else defend,
| And serving you so long!

| *Cleo.* I have one thing more to ask him yet, good Charmian:
| But 'tis no matter; thou shalt bring him to me
| Where I will write: All may be well enough.

| *Char.* I warrant you, madam.   [*Exeunt.*

Scene V—*A Room in* ANTONY'S *House*

III. v. 14. | *Eno.* Then, world, thou hast a pair of chaps, no more;
| And throw between them all the food thou hast,
| They'll grind the one the other. Where's Antony?

| *Eros.* He's walking in the garden—thus; and spurns
The rush that lies before him; cries, *Fool, Lepidus!*

Scene VI—*Rome. A Room in* CÆSAR'S *House*

Enter CÆSAR, AGRIPPA, *and* MECÆNAS

III. vi. 20.   *.Agr.* Who, queasy with his insolence

Enter OCTAVIA

III. vi. 42.   *Cæs.* Why have you stol'n upon us thus? You come not
| Like Cæsar's sister: The wife of Antony
| Should have an army for an usher, and
| The neighs of horse to tell of her approach,

| Long ere she did appear; the trees by the way,
| Should have borne men; and expectation fainted,
| Longing for what it had not: nay, the dust
| Should have ascended to the roof of heaven,
| Rais'd by your populous troops: But you are come
| A market-maid to Rome; and have prevented
| The ostent of our love, which, left unshown,
| Is often left unlov'd: we should have met you
| By sea, and land; supplying every stage
| With an augmented greeting.

III. vi. 65.   *Cæs.* No, my most wrong'd sister; Cleopatra
Hath nodded him to her. . . . . .

III. vi. 68.   . . . . He hath assembled
Bocchus, the king of Libya; Archelaus,
| Of Cappadocia; Philadelphos, king
| Of Paphlagonia; the Thracian king, Adallas;
| King Malchus of Arabia; King of Pont;
| Herod of Jewry; Mithridates, king
| Of Comagene; Polemon and Amintas,
| The kings of Mede, and Lycaonia, with a
| More larger list of sceptres.

III. vi. 84.   *Cæs.* But let determin'd things to destiny
Hold unbewail'd their way.

SCENE VII—ANTONY's *Camp, near the Promontory of Actium*

Enter a Soldier

III. vii. 61. | *Sold.* O noble emperor, do not fight by sea;
| Trust not to rotten planks: Do you misdoubt
| This sword, and these my wounds? Let the Egyptians,
| And the Phœnicians, go a-ducking; we
| Have us'd to conquer, standing on the earth,
| And fighting foot to foot.
        Ant.   Well, well,. away.
                [*Exeunt* ANTONY, CLEOPATRA, *and* ENOBARBUS.
    Sold. By Hercules, I think, I am i' the right.
    Can. Soldier, thou art: but his whole action grows

Not in the power on 't: So our leader's led,
And we are women's men.

SCENE VIII—*A Plain near Actium*
Enter SCARUS

III. viii. 19.　　*Scar.* On our side like the token'd pestilence,
Where death is sure.　Yon ribald-rid nag of Egypt,
Whom leprosy o'ertake! i' the midst o' the fight,—
When vantage like a pair of twins appear'd,
Both as the same, or rather ours the elder,—
The brize upon her, like a cow in June,
Hoists sails, and flies.
　　　　Eno.　　　　　　That I beheld: mine eyes
Did sicken at the sight on 't, and could not
Endure a further view.
　　　　Scar.　　　　　She once being loof'd,
The noble ruin of her magic, Antony,
Claps on his sea-wing, and like a doting mallard,
Leaving the fight in height, flies after her:
I never saw an action of such shame;
Experience, manhood, honour, ne'er before
Did violate so itself.
　　　　Eno.　　　　Alack, alack!

SCENE IX—*Alexandria. A Room in the Palace*
Enter ANTONY *and Attendants*

III. ix. 1.　|　*Ant.* Hark, the land bids me tread no more upon 't,
|It is asham'd to bear me!—Friends, come hither,
|I am so lated in the world, that I
|Have lost my way for ever:—I have a ship
|Laden with gold; take that, divide it; fly,
|And make your peace with Cæsar.
|　　*Att.*　　　　　　　　　　Fly! not we.
|　　*Ant.* I have fled myself; and have instructed cowards
|To run, and show their shoulders.—Friends, be gone;
|I have myself resolv'd upon a course,
|Which has no need of you; be gone:
|My treasure's in the harbour, take it.—O,
|I follow'd that I blush to look upon:

| My very hairs do mutiny; for the white
| Reprove the brown for rashness, and they them
| For fear and doting.—Friends, be gone; you shall
| Have letters from me to some friends, that will
| Sweep your way for you. Pray you, look not sad,
| Nor make replies of loathness: take the hint
| Which my despair proclaims; let that be left
| Which leaves itself: to the sea-side straightway:
| I will possess you of that ship and treasure.
| Leave me, I pray, a little: 'pray you now:—
| Nay, do so; for, indeed, I have lost command,
| Therefore I pray you:—I 'll see you by and by.

                                             [Sits down.

Enter EROS *and* CLEOPATRA, *led by* CHARMIAN *and* IRAS

III. ix. 28.   *Cleo.* Let me sit down. O Juno!

                Ant. No, no, no, no, no.

                Eros. See you here, sir?

                Ant. O fie, fie, fie.

                Char. Madam,—

                Iras. Madam; O good empress!—

                Eros. Sir, sir,—

                Ant. Yes, my lord, yes;—He, at Philippi, kept
His sword even like a dancer; while I struck
The lean and wrinkled Cassius; and 'twas I,
That the mad Brutus ended: he alone
Dealt on lieutenantry, and no practice had
In the brave squares of war: Yet now—No matter.

III. ix. 51.   *Ant.* O, whither hast thou led me, Egypt?

SCENE X—CÆSAR'S *Camp, in Egypt*

III. x. 3.   *Dol.* An argument that he is pluck'd, when hither
He sends so poor a pinion of his wing,

III. x. 8.   *Euph.* I was of late as petty to his ends,
As is the morn-dew on the myrtle leaf
To his grand sea.

Scene XI—*Alexandria*

Enter Cleopatra, Enobarbus, Charmian, *and* Iras

III. xi. 4.   *Eno.*   What although you fled
From that great face of war, whose several ranges
Frighted each other?

III. xi. 31.   *Eno.*   I see, men's judgements are
A parcel of their fortunes; and things outward
Do draw the inward quality after them,
To suffer all alike.

Enter an Attendant

III. xi. 37.   *Att.*   A messenger from Cæsar.
Cleo. What, no more ceremony?—See, my women!—
| Against the blown rose may they stop their nose,
| That kneel'd unto the buds.—Admit him, sir.   [*Exit* Attendant.

III. xi. 43.   *Eno.*   Yet, he, that can endure
To follow with allegiance a fallen lord,
Does conquer him that did his master conquer,
And earns a place i' the story.

Re-enter Antony *and* Enobarbus

III. xi. 85.   *Ant.*   Favours, by Jove that thunders!—

III. xi. 94. | *Eno.* 'Tis better playing with a lion's whelp,
| Than with an old one dying.

III. xi. 102. | *Ant.*   Tug him away: being whipp'd,
| Bring him again:—This Jack of Cæsar's shall
| Bear us an errand to him.—   [*Exeunt Att. with Thyr.*
| You were half blasted ere I knew you:—Ha!
| Have I my pillow left unpress'd in Rome,
| Forborne the getting of a lawful race,
| And by a gem of women, to be abus'd
| By one that looks on feeders?

III. xi. 111.   *Ant.* But when we in our viciousness grow hard,
(O misery on 't!) the wise gods seel our eyes;
In our own filth drop our clear judgements; make us

Adore our errors; laugh at us, while we strut
To our confusion.

III. xi. 116.   *Ant.* I found you as a morsel, cold upon
Dead Cæsar's trencher: .   .   .   .   .

III. xi. 120.   .   .   .   . For I am sure,
Though you can guess what temperance should be,
You know not what it is.

III. xi. 125.   *Ant.* My playfellow, your hand;   .   .   .   .   .

III. xi. 128.   .   .   .   . for I have savage cause;

III. xi. 145.   *Ant.* When my good stars, that were my former guides,
Have empty left their orbs, and shot their fires
Into the abysm of hell.

III. xi. 158.   *Cleo.*   Ah, dear, if I be so,
| From my cold heart let heaven engender hail,
| And poison it in the source; and the first stone
| Drop in my neck: as it determines, so
| Dissolve my life! The next Cæsarion smite!
| Till, by degrees, the memory of my womb,
| Together with my brave Egyptians all,
| By the discandying of this pelleted storm,
| Lie graveless: till the flies and gnats of Nile
| Have buried them for prey!

III. xi. 177. | *Ant.* I will be treble-sinew'd, hearted, breath'd,
| And fight maliciously: for when mine hours
| Were nice and lucky, men did ransom lives
| Of me for jests; but now I 'll set my teeth,
| And send to darkness all that stop me.—Come,
| Let 's have one other gaudy night: call to me
| All my sad captains, fill our bowls; once more
| Let 's mock the midnight bell.

III. xi. 189.   *Ant.*   and to-night I 'll force
The wine peep through their scars.

III. xi. 194.   *Eno.*   To be furious,
Is, to be frighted out of fear: and in that mood,

The dove will peck the estridge; and I see still,
A diminution in our captain's brain
Restores his heart: When valour preys on reason,
It eats the sword it fights with.

ACT IV

Scene I—Cæsar's *camp at Alexandria*

Enter Cæsar, *reading a Letter*; Agrippa, *and*
Mecænas, *and others*

IV. i. 1.   *Cæs.* He calls me boy; and chides, as he had power
To beat me out of Egypt: my messenger
He hath whipp'd with rods; dares me to personal combat,
Cæsar to Antony: Let the old ruffian know,
I have many other ways to die; mean time,
Laugh at his challenge.
    Mec.   Cæsar must think,
When one so great begins to rage, he 's hunted
Even to falling. Give him no breath, but now
Make boot of his distraction. Never anger
Made good guard for itself.
    Cæs.   Let our best heads
Know, that to-morrow the last of many battles
We mean to fight:—Within our files there are,
Of those that served Mark Antony but late,
Enough to fetch him in.

Scene II—*Alexandria. A Room in the Palace*

IV. ii. 14.   *Eno.* 'Tis one of those odd tricks, which sorrow shoots
Out of the mind.   [*Aside.*

IV. ii. 23.   *Cleo.*   What does he mean?
    Eno. To make his followers weep.
    Ant.   Tend me to-night;
May be, it is the period of your duty:
Haply, you shall not see me more; or if,
A mangled shadow: perchance, to-morrow
You 'll serve another master. I look on you,
As one that takes his leave. Mine honest friends,

| I turn you not away; but, like a master
| Married to your good service, stay till death:
| Tend me to-night two hours, I ask no more,
| And the gods yield you for 't!
| *Eno.*   What mean you, sir,
| To give them this discomfort? Look, they weep;
| And I, an ass, am onion-ey'd; for shame,

IV. ii. 40. | *Ant.* I spake to you for your comfort: did desire you
| To burn this night with torches: Know, my hearts,
| I hope well of to-morrow; and will lead you,
| Where rather I 'll expect victorious life,
| Than death and honour. Let 's to supper; come,
| And drown consideration.   [*Exeunt.*

SCENE IV—*The same. A Room in the Palace*

Enter EROS, *with Armour*

IV. iv. 5.   *Cleo.*   Nay, I 'll help too. |
What 's this for? |
   Ant.   Ah, let be, let be! thou art |
The armourer of my heart;—False, false; this, this. |
   Cleo. Sooth, la, I'll help: Thus it must be. |
   Ant.   Well, well; |
We shall thrive now.—See'st thou, my good fellow? |
Go, put on thy defences. |
   Eros.   Briefly, sir. |
   Cleo. Is not this buckled well? |
   Ant.   Rarely, rarely: |
He that unbuckles this, till we do please |
To doff't for our repose, shall hear a storm.— |
Thou fumblest, Eros; and my queen 's a squire |
More tight at this, than thou: Despatch.—O love, |
That thou couldst see my wars to-day, and knew'st |
The royal occupation! thou shouldst see |

Enter an Officer, armed |

A workman in 't.— |

IV. iv. 26.   *Ant.* This morning, like the spirit of a youth
That means to be of note, begins betimes.—

SCENE V—ANTONY'S *Camp near Alexandria*

IV. v. 12. | *Ant.* Go, Eros, send his treasure after; do it;
| Detain no jot, I charge thee: write to him
| (I will subscribe) gentle adieus, and greetings;
| Say, that I wish he never find more cause
| To change a master.—O, my fortunes have
| Corrupted honest men:—Eros, despatch.   [*Exeunt.*

SCENE VII—*Field of Battle between the Camps*

IV. vii. 7.   *Scar.* I had a wound here that was like a T,
But now 'tis made an H.

SCENE VIII—*Under the Walls of Alexandria*
Enter CLEOPATRA, *attended*

IV. viii. 14. | *Ant.* Chain my arm'd neck; leap thou, attire and all.
| Through proof of harness to my heart, and there
| Ride on the pants triumphing!

IV. viii. 28.   *Ant.* He has deserv'd it, were it carbuncled
Like holy Phœbus' car.   .   .   .   .

IV. viii. 32. | Had our great palace the capacity
| To camp this host, we all would sup together;
| And drink carouses to the next day's fate,
| Which promises royal peril.—Trumpeters,
| With brazen din blast you the city's ear;
| Make mingle with our rattling tabourines;
| That heaven and earth may strike their sounds together,
| Applauding our approach.   [*Exeunt.*

SCENE X—*Between the two Camps*

IV. x. 16.   *Scar.*   Swallows have built |
In Cleopatra's sails their nest: the augurers |
Say, they know not,—they cannot tell; look grimly, |
And dare not speak their knowledge. Antony |
Is valiant and dejected; and, by starts, |
His fretted fortunes give him hope, and fear, |
Of what he has, and has not. |
                    [*Alarum afar off, as at a Sea-fight.*

SCENE XII—*Alexandria. A Room in the Palace*

Enter ANTONY *and* EROS

IV. xii. 2.   *Ant.* Sometime, we see a cloud that 's dragonish;
A vapour, sometime, like a bear, or lion,
A tower'd citadel, a pendant rock,
A forked mountain, or blue promontory
With trees upon 't, that nod unto the world,
And mock our eyes with air: Thou hast seen these signs;
They are black vesper's pageants.
     Eros.   Ay, my lord.
    Ant. That, which is now a horse, even with a thought,
The rack dislimns; and makes it indistinct,
As water is in water.

IV. xii. 57.   *Ant.*   I, that with my sword
Quarter'd the world, and o'er green Neptune's back
With ships made cities, condemn myself, to lack
The courage of a woman; less noble mind
Than she, which, by her death, our Cæsar tells,
I am conqueror of myself.

IV. xii. 71.   *Ant.*   Eros,
Wouldst thou be window'd in great Rome, and see
Thy master thus with pleach'd arms, bending down
His corrigible neck, his face subdued
To penetrative shame,

IV. xii. 99.   *Ant.*   But I will be
A bridegroom in my death, and run into 't
As to a lover's bed. Come then;

SCENE XIII—*The same. A Monument*

Enter ANTONY, *borne by the Guard*

IV. xiii. 9.   *Cleo.*   O thou sun,
Burn the great sphere thou mov'st in!—darkling stand,
The varying shore o' the world!—O Antony!
Antony, Antony!—Charmian, help; help, Iras;
Help, friends below; let 's draw him hither.

| *Ant.*   Peace:
| Not Cæsar's valour hath o'erthrown Antony,
| But Antony's hath triumph'd on itself.
| *Cleo.* So it should be, that none but Antony
| Should conquer Antony; but woe 'tis so!
| *Ant.* I am dying, Egypt, dying; only
| I here impórtune death awhile, until
| Of many thousand kisses the poor last
| I lay upon thy lips.—

IV. xiii. 41.   *Ant.* I am dying, Egypt, dying:

IV. xiii. 63. | *Cleo.* The crown o' the earth doth melt:—My lord!—
| O, wither'd is the garland of the war,
| The soldiers' pole is fallen; young boys, and girls,
| Are level now with men: the odds is gone,
| And there is nothing left remarkable
| Beneath the visiting moon.   [*She faints.*
| *Char.*   O, quietness, lady!

IV. xiii. 80.   *Cleo.*   Then is it sin,
To rush into the secret house of death,
Ere death dare come to us?

IV. xiii. 87.   *Cleo.* Let 's do it after the high Roman fashion,
And make death proud to take us.

ACT V

Scene I—Cæsar's *Camp before Alexandria*

V. i. 14. | *Cæs.* The breaking of so great a thing should make
| A greater crack: The round world should have shook
| Lions into civil streets,
| And citizens to their dens:—The death of Antony
| Is not a single doom; in the name lay
| A moiety of the world.
| *Der.*   He is dead, Cæsar;
| Not by a public minister of justice,
| Nor by a hired knife; but that self hand,
| Which writ his honour in the acts it did,
| Hath, with the courage which the heart did lend it,

| Splitted the heart.—This is his sword,
| I robb'd his wound of it; behold it stain'd
| With his most noble blood.

SCENE II—*Alexandria. A Room in the Monument*

V. ii. 55. | *Cleo.*   Shall they hoist me up,
| And show me to the shouting varletry
| Of censuring Rome? Rather a ditch in Egypt
| Be gentle grave to me! rather on Nilus' mud
| Lay me stark naked, and let the water-flies
| Blow me into abhorring! rather make
| My country's high pyramids my gibbet,
| And hang me up in chains!
| *Pro.*   You do extend
| These thoughts of horror further than you shall
| Find cause in Cæsar.

V. ii. 74. | *Cleo.* You laugh, when boys, or women, tell their dreams;
| Is 't not your trick?

V. ii. 82.   *Cleo.* His legs bestrid the ocean: his rear'd arm
Crested the world: his voice was propertied
As all the tuned spheres, and that to friends;
But when he meant to quail and shake the orb,
He was as rattling thunder. For his bounty,
There was no winter in 't; an autumn 'twas,
That grew the more by reaping: His delights
Were dolphin-like; they show'd his back above
The element they liv'd in: In his livery
Walk'd crowns and crownets; realms and islands were
As plates dropp'd from his pocket.
        Dol.   Cleopatra,— |
        Cleo. Think you, there was, or might be, such a man |
As this I dream'd of? |
        Dol.   Gentle madam, no. |
        Cleo. You lie, up to the hearing of the gods. |
But, if there be, or ever were one such, |
It 's past the size of dreaming: Nature wants stuff |
To vie strange forms with fancy; yet, to imagine |

An Antony, were nature's piece 'gainst fancy,
Condemning shadows quite.
    Dol.   Hear me, good madam:
Your loss is as yourself, great; and you bear it
As answering to the weight: 'Would I might never
O'ertake pursu'd success, but I do feel,
By the rebound of yours, a grief that shoots
My very heart at root.

V. ii. 157.   *Cæs.*   Good queen, let us entreat you.
    Cleo. O Cæsar, what a wounding shame is this;
That thou, vouchsafing here to visit me,
Doing the honour of thy lordliness
To one so meek, that mine own servant should
Parcel the sum of my disgraces by
Addition of his envy! Say, good Cæsar,
That I some lady trifles have reserv'd,
Immoment toys, things of such dignity
As we greet modern friends withal: and say,
Some nobler token I have kept apart
For Livia, and Octavia, to induce
Their mediation; must I be unfolded
With one that I have bred? <u>The gods!</u> it smites me
<u>Beneath the fall I have.</u>

V. ii. 204.   *Dol.*   I your servant.
Adieu, good queen; I must attend on Cæsar.
    Cleo. Farewell, and thanks.   [*Exit* Dol.
                     Now, Iras, what think'st thou?
Thou, an Egyptian puppet, shalt be shown
In Rome, as well as I: mechanic slaves
With greasy aprons, rules, and hammers, shall
Uplift us to the view; in their thick breaths,
Rank of gross diet, shall we be enclouded,
And forc'd to drink their vapour.
    Iras.   The gods forbid!
    Cleo. Nay, 'tis most certain, Iras: Saucy lictors
Will catch at us, like strumpets; and scald rhymers
Ballad us out o' tune: the quick comedians
Extemporally will stage us, and present

| Our Alexandrian revels; Antony
| Shall be brought drunken forth, and I shall see
| Some squeaking Cleopatra boy my greatness
| I' the posture of a whore.
| *Iras.*   O the good gods!
| *Cleo.* Nay, that's certain.
| *Iras.* I'll never see it; for, I am sure, my nails
| Are stronger than mine eyes.
| *Cleo.*   Why, that's the way
| To fool their preparation, and to conquer
| Their most absurd intents.—Now, Charmian?—

| *Enter* CHARMIAN
| Show me, my women, like a queen;—Go fetch
| My best attires;—I am again for Cydnus,
| To meet Mark Antony:—Sirrah—Iras, go.
| Now, noble Charmian, we'll despatch indeed:
| And, when thou hast done this chare, I'll give thee leave
| To play till doomsday.—Bring our crown and all.
| Wherefore's this noise?   [*Exit* IRAS. *A Noise within.*

| *Re-enter* Guard, *with a* Clown *bringing a Basket*
V. ii. 240. | *Guard.*   This is the man.
| *Cleo.* Avoid, and leave him.   [*Exit* Guard.
| Hast thou the pretty worm of Nilus there,
| That kills and pains not?
| *Clown.* Truly, I have him: but I would not be the party that
| should desire you to touch him, for his biting is immortal; those
| that do die of it, do seldom or never recover.
| *Cleo.* Remember'st thou any that have died on't?
| *Clown.* Very many, men and women too. I heard of one of
| them no longer than yesterday: a very honest woman, but some-
| thing given to lie; as a woman should not do, but in the way of
| honesty: how she died of the biting of it, what pain she felt.—
| Truly, she makes a very good report o' the worm: But he that will
| believe all that they say, shall never be saved by half that they do:
| But this is most fallible, the worm's an odd worm.
| *Cleo.* Get thee hence; farewell.
| *Clown.* I wish you all joy of the worm.
| [Clown *sets down the Basket.*

V. ii. 261. | *Cleo.* Farewell.

| *Clown.* You must think this, look you, that the worm will do
| his kind.

| *Cleo.* Ay, ay; farewell.

| *Clown.* Look you, the worm is not to be trusted, but in the
| keeping of wise people; for, indeed, there is no goodness in the
| worm.

| *Cleo.* Take thou no care; it shall be heeded.

| *Clown.* Very good: give it nothing, I pray you, for it is not
| worth the feeding.

| *Cleo.* Will it eat me?

| *Clown.* You must not think I am so simple, but I know the devil
| himself will not eat a woman: I know, that a woman is a dish for
| the gods, if the devil dress her not. But, truly, these same whoreson
| devils do the gods great harm in their women; for in every ten
| that they make, the devils mar five.

| *Cleo.* Well, get thee gone; farewell.

| *Clown.* Yes, forsooth; I wish you joy of the worm.   [*Exit.*

Re-enter IRAS, *with a Robe, Crown, &c.*

Cleo. Give me my robe, put on my crown; I have |
Immortal longings in me: Now no more |
The juice of Egypt's grape shall moist this lip:— |
Yare, yare, good Iras; quick.—Methinks, I hear |
Antony call; I see him rouse himself |
To praise my noble act; I hear him mock |
The luck of Cæsar, which the gods give men |
To excuse their after wrath: Husband, I come: |
Now to that name my courage prove my title! |
I am fire, and air; my other elements |
I give to baser life.—So,—have you done? |
Come then, and take the last warmth of my lips. |
Farewell, kind Charmian;—Iras, long farewell. |

                    [*Kisses them.* IRAS *falls and dies.* |

Have I the aspic in my lips? Dost fall? |
If thou and nature can so gently part, |
The stroke of death is as a lover's pinch, |
Which hurts, and is desir'd. Dost thou lie still? |
If thus thou vanishest, thou tell'st the world |
It is not worth leave-taking. |

Char. Dissolve, thick cloud, and rain; that I may say
The gods themselves do weep!
    Cleo.   This proves me base:
If she first meet the curled Antony,
He'll make demand of her; and spend that kiss,
Which is my heaven to have.—Come, mortal wretch.
                [To the Asp, which she applies to her Breast.
With thy sharp teeth this knot intrinsicate
Of life at once untie: poor venomous fool,
Be angry, and despatch. O, couldst thou speak!
That I might hear thee call great Cæsar, ass
Unpolicied!
    Char.   O eastern star!
    Cleo.   Peace, peace!
Dost thou not see my baby at my breast,
That sucks the nurse asleep?
    Char.   O, break! O, break!
    Cleo. As sweet as balm, as soft as air, as gentle,—
O Antony!—Nay, I will take thee too:—
             [Applying another Asp to her Arm.
What, should I stay—   *[Falls on a Bed and dies.*
    Char. In this wild world?—So, fare thee well.—
Now boast thee, death! in thy possession lies
A lass unparallel'd.—Downy windows, close;
And golden Phœbus never be beheld
Of eyes again so royal! Your crown's awry;
I'll mend it, and then play.

            Enter DOLABELLA

V. ii. 343.   *First Guard.* I found her trimming up the diadem
On her dead mistress; tremblingly she stood,
And on the sudden dropp'd.
    Cæs.   O noble weakness!—
If they had swallow'd poison, 'twould appear
By external swelling: but she looks like sleep,
As she would catch another Antony
In her strong toil of grace.
    Dol.   Here, on her breast,
There is a vent of blood, and something blown:
The like is on her arm.

First Guard. This is an aspic's trail: and these fig-leaves
Have slime upon them, such as the aspic leaves
Upon the caves of Nile.
    Cæs.   Most probable,
That so she died; for her physician tells me,
She hath pursu'd conclusions infinite
Of easy ways to die.—Take up her bed;
And bear her women from the monument:—
She shall be buried by her Antony:

The following is an accurate reprint of all Keats's marks and notes in the text of *Troilus and Cressida* in the 1808 reprint of the 1623 folio edition, now in the Dilke Collection at Hampstead.

TROILUS AND CRESSIDA

THE PROLOGUE

l. 12.   *And the deepe-drawing Barke do there disgorge*
        Their warlike frautage:

l. 17.   *And* Antenonidus *with massie Staples*
        And corresponsiue and fulfilling Bolts
        Stirre vp the Sonnes of Troy.
        Now Expectation tickling skittish spirits,

l. 27.   *our Play*
        Leapes ore the vaunt and firstlings of those broyles,

ACTUS PRIMUS. SCENA PRIMA

Enter PANDARUS *and* TROYLUS

I. i. 9.   *Troy.* But I am weaker then a womans teare;
      Tamer then sleepe, fonder then ignorance;
      Lesse valiant then the Virgin in the night,
      And skillesse as vnpractis'd Infancie.

I. i. 29.   *Troy.* Patience her selfe, what Goddesse ere she be,
      Doth lesser blench at sufferance, then I doe:

I. i. 39.   * *Troy.* I haue (as when the Sunne doth light a-scorne)
      Buried this sigh, in wrinkle of a smile:

KEATS'S NOTE] *I have not read this copy much and yet have had time to find many faults—however 'tis certain that the Commentators have contrived to twist many beautiful passages into common places as they have done with respect to "a scorn" which they have hocus pocus'd in[to] " a storm " thereby destroying the depth of the simile–taking away all the surrounding Atmosphere of Imagery and leaving a bare and unapt picture. Now however beautiful a comparison may be for a bare aptness–Shakspeare is seldom guilty of one–he could not be content to the " sun lighting a storm", but he gives us Apollo in the act of drawing back his head and forcing a smile upon the world—'the Sun doth light a-scorn ".

I. i. 50.

Troy. Oh *Pandarus*! I tell thee *Pandarus*;

When I doe tell thee, ^wthere * my hopes lye drown'd:
Reply not in how many Fadomes deepe
They lye indrench'd. I tell thee, I am mad
In *Cressids* loue. Thou answer'st she is Faire,
Powr'st in the open Vlcer of my heart,
Her Eyes, her Haire, her Cheeke, her Gate, her Voice,
Handlest in thy discourse.

I. i. 59.

                   to whose soft seizure,
The Cignets Downe is harsh, and spirit of Sense
Hard as the palme of Plough-man.

I. i. 66.

Pan. I speake no more then truth.
Troy. Thou do'st not speake so much.

I. i. 98.

Troy. It is too staru'd a subiect for my Sword,

.   .   .   .   .   .

I. i. 101.

And he 's as teachy to be woo'd to woe,

.   .   .   .   .   .

I. i. 105.

Her bed is *India*, there she lies, a Pearle,
Between our Ilium, and where shee recides
Let it be cald the wild and wandring flood,
Our selfe the Merchant, and this sayling *Pandar*,
Our doubtfull hope, our conuoy and our Barke.

Enter CRESSID *and her man*

I. ii. 4.

Man.   *Hector* whose pacience,
Is as a Vertue fixt, to day was mou'd.

.   .   .   .   .   .

I. ii. 9.

And to the field goe's he; where euery flower
Did as a Prophet weepe what it forsaw,
In *Hectors* wrath.

I. ii. 15.

Man. They say he is a very man *per se* and stands alone.

I. ii. 30.

Man. hee is a gowtie *Briareus*, many hands and no vse; or pur-
blinded *Argus*, all eyes and no sight.

* w for t; Keats's script.

I. ii. 112.   *Cre.* I had as lieue <u>*Hellens* golden tongue</u> had commended
Troylus for a copper nose.

I. ii. 116.   *Cre.* <u>Then shee 's a merry Greeke indeed.</u>

I. ii. 128.   *Pan.* But to prooue to you that *Hellen* loues him, she came
<u>and puts me her white hand to his clouen chin.</u>
    *   *Cres.* <u>*Iuno* haue mercy,</u> how came it clouen?

I. ii. 186.   *Pand.* Ile be sworne 'tis true, <u>he will weepe you an'twere</u>
<u>a man borne in Aprill.</u>   *Sound a retreate.*
    Cres. <u>And Ile spring vp in his teares, an'twere a nettle against</u>
<u>May.</u>

I. ii. 272.   *Pan.* Do you know what a man is? Is not birth, beauty, good
shape, discourse, manhood, learning, gentlenesse, vertue, youth,
liberality, and so forth: <u>the Spice, and salt that seasons a man?</u>

I. ii. 310.   *Cres.* Women are Angels wooing,
Things won are done, <u>ioyes soule lyes in the dooing:</u>

      Senet. Enter AGAMEMNON, NESTOR, VLYSSES, DIOMEDES,
             MENELAUS, *with others*

I. iii. 1.   *Agam.* Princes:
<u>What greefe hath set the Iaundies on your cheekes?</u>

I. iii. 5.   . . . . <u>checkes and disasters</u>
<u>Grow in the veines of actions highest rear'd.</u>
<u>As knots by the conflux of meeting sap,</u>
<u>Infect the sound Pine, and diuerts his Graine</u>
<u>Tortiue and erant from his course of growth.</u>
      .   .   .   .

I. iii. 13.   † <u>Sith euery action that hath gone before,</u>
<u>Whereof we haue Record, Triall did draw</u>
<u>Bias and thwart, not answering the ayme:</u>

KEATS'S NOTE] * A most delicate touch—Juno being the Goddess of Childbirth.

KEATS'S NOTE] † The Genius of Shakspeare was an in[n]ate universality–wherefore
he had the utmost atchievement of human intellect prostrate beneath his indolent and kingly
gaze. He could do easily Man's utmost. His plans of tasks to come were not of this world—
if what he purposed to do here after would not in his own Idea ' answer the aim ' how
tremendous must have been his Conception of Ultimates.

And that vnbodied figure of the thought
That gaue 't surmised shape. . . . . .

I. iii. 19.   . . . . which are (indeed) nought else
But the protractiue trials of great Ioue,
To finde persistiue constancie in men?
The finenesse of which Mettall is not found
In Fortunes loue: for then, the Bold and Coward,
The Wise and Foole, the Artist and vn-read,
The hard and soft, seeme all affin'd, and kin.
But in the Winde and Tempest of her frowne,
| Distinction with a lowd and powrefull fan,
| Puffing at all, winnowes the light away;
| And what hath masse, or matter by it selfe,
| Lies rich in Vertue, and vnmingled.
    Nestor. With due Obseruance of thy godly seat,
Great *Agamemnon*, *Nestor* shall apply
Thy latest words.
In the reproofe of Chance,
Lies the true proofe of men: The Sea being smooth,
How many shallow bauble Boates dare saile
Vpon her patient brest, making their way
With those of Nobler bulke?
But let the Ruffian *Boreas* once enrage
The gentle *Thetis*, and anon behold
The strong ribb'd Barke through liquid Mountaines cut,
Bounding betweene the two moyst Elements
Like *Perseus* Horse. Where 's then the sawcy Boate,
Whose weake vntimber'd sides but euen now
Co-riual'd Greatnesse? Either to harbour fled,
Or made a Toste for Neptune. Euen so,
Doth valours shew, and valours worth diuide
In stormes of Fortune.
For, in her ray and brightnesse,
The Heard hath more annoyance by the Brieze
Then by the Tyger: But, when the splitting winde
Makes flexible the knees of knotted Oakes,
And Flies fled vnder shade, why then
The thing of Courage,
As rowz'd with rage, with rage doth sympathize,

And with an accent tun'd in selfe-same key,
Retyres to chiding Fortune.
   Vlys. Agamemnon:
Thou great Commander, Nerue, and Bone of Greece,
.   .   .   .

I. iii. 61.   And thou most reuerend for thy stretcht-out life,
I giue to both your speeches: which were such,
As *Agamemnon* and the hand of Greece
Should hold vp high in Brasse: and such againe
As venerable *Nestor* (hatch'd in Siluer)
| Should with a bond of ayre, strong as the Axletree
| In which the Heauens ride, knit all Greekes eares
| To his experienc'd tongue:

I. iii. 74.   *Aga.* We shall heare Musicke, Wit, and Oracle.

I. iii. 79.   *Vlys.* And looke how many Grecian Tents do stand
Hollow vpon this Plaine, so many hollow Factions.
When that the Generall is not like the Hiue,
To whom the Forragers shall all repaire,
What Hony is expected? Degree being vizarded,
Th'vnworthiest shewes as fairely in the Maske.
The Heauens themselues, the Planets, and this Center,
Obserue degree, priority, and place,
Insisture, course, proportion, season, forme,
Office, and custome, in all line of Order:
And therefore is the glorious Planet Sol
In noble eminence, enthron'd and sphear'd
Amid'st the other, whose med'cinable eye
Corrects the ill Aspects of Planets euill,
And postes like the Command'ment of a King,
Sans checke, to good and bad. . . .

I. iii. 98.   .   .   .   . Frights, changes, horrors,
Diuert, and cracke, rend and deracinate
The vnity, and married calme of States
Quite from their fixure? . . . . .

I. iii. 103.   .   .   .   .   . How could Communities,
.   .   .   .

I. iii. 106.   The primogenitiue, and due of Byrth,
Prerogatiue of Age, Crownes, Scepters, Lawrels,
(But by Degree) stand in Authentique place?
Take but Degrèe away, vn-tune that string,
And hearke what Discord followes: each thing meetes
In meere oppugnancie. The bounded Waters,
Should lift their bosomes higher then the Shores,
And make a soppe of all this solid Globe:

I. iii. 116.   . . . . right and wrong,
(Betweene whose endlesse iarre, Iustice recides)
Should loose her names, and so should Iustice too.
Then euery thing includes it selfe in Power,
Power into Will, Will into Appetite,
And Appetite (an vniuersall Wolfe,
So doubly seconded with Will, and Power)
Must make perforce an vniuersall prey,
And last, eate vp himselfe.
Great *Agamemnon*:
This Chaos, when Degree is suffocate,
Followes the choaking:
And this neglection of Degree, is it
That by a pace goes backward in a purpose
It hath to climbe. . . . .

I. iii. 133.   . . . . . . growes to an enuious Feauer
Of pale, and bloodlesse Emulation.

I. iii. 142.   *Vlys.* The great *Achilles*, whom Opinion crownes,
The sinew, and the fore-hand of our Hoste,
Hauing his eare full of his ayery Fame,
Growes dainty of his worth, and in his Tent
Lyes mocking our designes. With him, *Patroclus*,
Vpon a lazie Bed, the liue-long day
Breakes scurrill Iests,
And with ridiculous and aukward action,
(Which Slanderer, he imitation call's)
He Pageants vs. Sometime great *Agamemnon*,
Thy toplesse deputation he puts on;
And like a strutting Player, whose conceit

Lies in his Ham-string, and doth thinke it rich
To heare the woodden Dialogue and sound
'Twixt his stretcht footing, and the Scaffolage,
Such to be pittied, and ore-rested seeming
He acts thy Greatnesse in: and when he speakes,
'Tis like a Chime a mending. With tearmes vnsquar'd,
Which from the tongue of roaring *Typhon* dropt,
Would seemes Hyperboles. At this fusty stuffe,
The large *Achilles* (on his prest-bed lolling)
From his deepe Chest, laughes out a lowd applause,
Cries excellent, 'tis *Agamemnon* iust.
Now play me *Nestor*; hum, and stroke thy Beard
As he, being drest to some Oration:
That's done, as neere as the extreamest ends
Of paralels; as like, as *Vulcan* and his wife,
.   .   .   .

I. iii. 172.   And then (forsooth) the faint defects of Age
Must be the Scene of myrth, to cough, and spit,
And with a palsie fumbling on his Gorget,
Shake in and out the Riuet: and at this sport
Sir Valour dies; cries, O enough *Patroclus*,
Or, giue me ribs of Steele, I shall split all
In pleasure of my Spleene.   .   .   .   .

I. iii. 183.   .   .   .   .   what is, or is not, serues
As stuffe for these two, to make paradoxes.
Nest. And in the imitation of these twaine,
Who (as *Vlysses* sayes) Opinion crownes
With an Imperiall voyce, many are infect:
Aiax is growne selfe-will'd, and beares his head
In such a reyne in full as proud a place
As broad *Achilles*, and keepes his Tent like him;
Makes factious Feasts, railes on our state of Warre
Bold as an Oracle, and sets *Thersites*
A slaue, whose Gall coines slanders like a Mint,
To match vs in comparisons with durt,

I. iii. 202.   *Vlys.*   and know by measure
Of their obseruant toyle, the Enemies waight,
Why this hath not a fingers dignity:

They call this Bed-worke, Mapp'ry, Closset-Warre:
So that the Ramme that batters downe the wall,
For the great swing and rudenesse of his poize,
They place before his hand that made the Engine,
Or those that with the finenesse of their soules,
By Reason guide his execution.

    Nest. Let this be granted, and *Achilles* horse
Makes many Thetis sonnes.

                                      Quey *
                                      Tucket.

I. iii. 218.   *Æne.* May one that is a Herald, and a Prince,
Do a faire message to his Kingly eares?

I. iii. 228.   *Æne.*   a blush
Modest as morning, when she coldly eyes
The youthfull Phœbus:

I. iii. 235.   *Æne.* Courtiers as free, as debonnaire; vnarm'd,
As bending Angels: that's their Fame, in peace:
But when they would seeme Souldiers, they haue galles,
Good armes, strong ioynts, true swords, & *Ioues* accord,

I. iii. 251.   *Æne.* I bring a Trumpet to awake his eare,
To set his sence on the attentiue bent,
And then to speake.

I. iii. 256.   *Æne.* Trumpet blow loud,
Send thy Brasse voyce through all these lazie Tents,
And euery Greeke of mettle, let him know,
What Troy meanes fairely, shall be spoke alowd.
                                    The Trumpets sound.
We haue great *Agamemnon* heere in Troy,
A Prince calld *Hector*, *Priam* is his Father:
Who in this dull and long-continew'd Truce
Is rusty growne. He bad me take a Trumpet,
And to this purpose speake: Kings, Princes, Lords,
If there be one among'st the fayr'st of Greece,
That holds his Honor higher then his ease,
That seekes his praise, more then he feares his perill,
That knowes his Valour, and knowes not his feare,

* Keats's script.

That loues his Mistris more then in confession,

. . . .

I. iii. 280. | If any come, *Hector* shal honour him:
              | If none, hee'l say in Troy when he retyres,
              The Grecian Dames are sun-burnt, and not worth
              The splinter of a Lance: Euen so much.
                 Aga. This shall be told our Louers Lord *Æneas*,
              If none of them haue soule in such a kinde,
              We left them all at home:

I. iii. 291.   *Nest.* Tell him of *Nestor*, one that was a man
              When *Hectors* Grandsire suckt: he is old now,

I. iii. 295. . . . . tell him from me,
              Ile hide my Siluer beard in a Gold Beauer,
              And in my Vantbrace put this wither'd brawne,
              And meeting him, wil tell him, that my Lady
              Was fayrer then his Grandame, and as chaste
              As may be in the world:

I. iii. 312.   *Vlys.* I haue a young conception in my braine,
              Be you my time to bring it to some shape.

I. iii. 316. | *Vlysses.* Blunt wedges riue hard knots: the seeded Pride
              | That hath to this maturity blowne vp *
              In ranke *Achilles*, must or now be cropt,
              Or shedding breed a Nursery of like euil
              ‖ To ouer-bulke vs all.
                 Nest. Wel, and how?
              | *Vlys.* This challenge that the gallant *Hector* sends,
              | How euer it is spred in general name,
              | Relates in purpose onely to *Achilles*.
                 Nest. The purpose is perspicuous euen as substance,
              Whose grossenesse little charracters summe vp,
              And in the publication make no straine,
              But that *Achilles*, were his braine as barren
              As bankes of Lybia,

KEATS'S NOTE] * "Blowne up" etc. One's very breath while leaning over these Pages is held for fear of blowing this line away—as easily as the gentlest breeze~~despoils~~ Robs dandelions of their fleecy Crowns.

I. iii. 337.   *Nest.* For heere the Troyans taste our deer'st repute
                With their fin'st Pallate: . . . . .

I. iii. 343.   And in such Indexes, although small prickes
                To their subsequent Volumes, there is seene
                The baby figure of the Gyant-masse
                Of things to come at large. It is suppos'd,
                He that meets *Hector*, issues from our choyse;
                And choise being mutuall acte of all our soules,
                Makes Merit her election, and doth boyle
                As 'twere, from forth vs all: a man distill'd
                Out of our Vertues; who miscarrying,
                What heart from hence receyues the conqu'ring part
                To steele a strong opinion to themselues? *
                Which entertain'd, Limbes are in his instruments,   Que^y †
                In no lesse working, then are Swords and Bowes
                Directiue by the Limbes.

I. iii. 370.   *Vlys.* And we were better parch in Affricke Sunne,
                Then in the pride and salt scorne of his eyes
       .   .   .   .

I. iii. 378.   For that will physicke the great Myrmidon
                Who broyles in lowd applause, and make him fall
                His Crest, that prouder then blew Iris bends.
                If the dull brainlesse *Aiax* come safe off,
                Wee'l dresse him vp in voyces:

               Enter AIAX *and* THERSITES

II. i. 14.   *Ther.* The plague of Greece vpon thee: thou Mungrel beefe-
                witted Lord.

II. i. 42. | *Ther.* He would pun thee into shiuers with his fist, as a Sailor
              | breakes a bisket.

II. i. 134.   *Achil.* That *Hector* by the fift houre of the Sunne,

          Enter PRIAM, HECTOR, TROYLUS, PARIS *and* HELENUS
II. ii. 8. | *Hect.* Though no man lesser feares the Greeks then I,
             | As farre as touches my particular: yet dread *Priam*,

       * Query mark added by Keats.   † Keats's script.

| There is no Lady of more softer bowels,
| More spungie, to sucke in the sense of Feare,
| More ready to cry out, who knowes what followes
| Then *Hector* is: the wound of peace is surety,
| Surety secure: but modest Doubt is cal'd
| The Beacon of the wise: the tent that searches
| To' th' bottome of the worst.

II. ii. 25.   *Troy.* Fie, fie, my Brother;
Weigh you the worth and honour of a King
(So great as our dread Father) in a Scale
Of common Ounces? Wil you with Counters summe
The past proportion of his infinite,
And buckle in a waste most fathomlesse,
With spannes and inches so diminutiue,
As feares and reasons? Fie for godly shame?

II. ii. 37.   *Troy.* You are for dreames & slumbers brother Priest
You furre your gloues with reason:
· · · · · · · ·

II. ii. 46.   Or like a Starre disorb'd. Nay, if we talke of Reason,
And flye like chidden Mercurie from Ioue,
Let's shut our gates and sleepe:

II. ii. 52.   *Troy.* What's aught, but as 'tis valew'd?

II. ii. 75.   *Troy.* The Seas and Windes (old Wranglers) tooke a Truce,
And did him seruice; he touch'd the Ports desir'd,
And for an old Aunt whom the Greekes held Captiue,
He brought a Grecian Queen, whose youth & freshnesse
Wrinkles *Apolloes*, and makes stale the morning.
Why keepe we her? the Grecians keepe our Aunt:
Is she worth keeping? Why she is a Pearle,
Whose price hath launch'd aboue a thousand Ships,
And turn'd Crown'd Kings to Merchants.

II. ii. 105.   *Cas.* Soft infancie, that nothing can but cry,

II. ii. 127.   *Troy.* And Ioue forbid there should be done among'st vs
Such things as might offend the weakest spleene,
To fight for, and maintaine.

II. ii. 132.   *Par.* But I attest the gods, your full consent
Gaue wings to my propension, and cut off
All feares attending on so dire a proiect.
For what (alas) can these my single armes?
What propugnation is in one mans valour
To stand the push and enmity of those
This quarrel would excite?

II. ii. 142.   *Pri. Paris*, you speake
Like one be-sotted on your sweet delights;
You haue the Hony still but these the Gall,
So to be valiant, is no praise at all.
        Par. Sir, I propose not meerely to my selfe,
The pleasures such a beauty brings with it:
But I would haue the soyle of her faire Rape
Wip'd off in honourable keeping her.
What Treason were it to the ransack'd Queene,
Disgrace to your great worths, and shame to me,
Now to deliuer her possession vp
On termes of base compulsion? Can it be,
That so degenerate a straine as this,
Should once set footing in your generous bosomes?
There 's not the meanest spirit on our partie,
Without a heart to dare, or sword to draw,
When *Helen* is defended: nor none so Noble,
Whose life were ill bestow'd, or death vnfam'd,
Where *Helen* is the subiect. Then (I say)
Well may we fight for her, whom we know well,
The worlds large spaces cannot paralell.

II. ii. 168.   *Hect.* The Reasons you alledge, do more conduce
To the hot passion of distemp'red blood,
Then to make up a free determination
'Twixt right and wrong: For pleasure, and reuenge,
Haue eares more deafe then Adders, to the voyce
Of any true decision.

II. ii. 194.   *Tro.* Why? there you toucht the life of our designe:
Were it not glory that we more affected,
Then the performance of our heauing spleenes,

I would not with a drop of *Troian* blood,
Spent more in her defence. <u>But worthy *Hector*,</u>
<u>She is a theame of honour and renowne,</u>
<u>A spurre to valiant and magnanimous deeds,</u>
<u>Whose present courage may beate downe our foes,</u>
<u>And fame in time to come canonize vs.</u>

Enter THERSITES *solus*

II. iii. 12.   *Ther.* and *Mercury*, loose all <u>the Serpentine craft of thy</u>
<u>Caduceus,</u> . . . .

II. iii. 17.   <u>it will not in circumuention deliuer a Flye from a Spider,</u>

II. iii. 30.   *Ther.* The common curse of mankinde, follie and ignorance
be thine in great reuenew; heauen blesse thee from a Tutor, and
Discipline come not neere thee.

II. iii. 43.   *Achil.* Where, where, art thou come? why my cheese, my
digestion, why hast thou not seru'd thy selfe into my Table,
so many meales? Come, what's *Agamemnon?*

II. iii. 87.   *Agam.* He sent our Messengers, and we lay by
Our <u>appertainments,</u> visiting of him:

II. iii. 94.   *Aia.* Yes, <u>Lyon sicke, sicke of proud heart; you may call it</u>
<u>Melancholly if will fauour the man, but by my head, it is pride;</u>

II. iii. 114.   *Vlis.* <u>The Elephant hath ioynts, but none for curtesie:</u>

II. iii. 124.   *Aga.* <u>But his euasion winged thus swift with scorne,</u>
<u>Cannot outflye our apprehensions.</u>
Much attribute he hath, and much the reason,
Why we ascribe it to him, yet all his vertues,
Not vertuously of his owne part beheld,
Doe in our eyes, begin to loose their glosse:
Yea, and like faire Fruit in an vnholdsome dish,
Are like to rot vntasted: goe and tell him,
We came to speake with him; <u>and you shall not sinne,</u>
<u>If you doe say, we thinke him ouer proud,</u>
<u>And vnder honest;</u> . . . . .

II. iii. 138. And vnder write in an obseruing kinde
His humorous predominance, yea watch
His pettish lines, his ebs, his flowes, as if
The passage and whole carriage of this action
Rode on his tyde.

II. iii. 162. *Aiax.* Why should a man be proud? How doth pride grow?
I know not what it is.

II. iii. 175. *Vlis.* He doth relye on none,
But carries on the streame of his dispose,
Without obseruance or respect of any,
In will peculiar, and in selfe admission.
  Aga. Why, will he not vpon our faire request,
Vntent his person, and share the ayre with vs?
  Vlis. Things small as nothing, for requests sake onely
He makes important; possest he is with greatnesse,
And speakes not to himselfe, but with a pride
That quarrels at selfe-breath. Imagin'd wroth
Holds in his bloud such swolne and hot discourse,
That twixt his mentall and his actiue parts,
Kingdom'd *Achilles* in commotion rages,
And batters gainst it selfe;

II. iii. 208. *Vlis.* And adde more Coles to Cancer, when he burnes
With entertaining great *Hiperion.*

II. iii. 212. *Nest.* O this is well, he rubs the veine of him.
  Dio. And how his silence drinkes vp this applause.

II. iii. 254. *Vl.* Thank the heauens L. thou art of sweet composure;

II. iii. 261. *Vl.* Bull-bearing *Milo*: his addition yeelde
To sinnowie *Aiax*: . . . . . .

II. iii. 264. . . . . here's *Nestor*
Instructed by the Antiquary Times: |||
. . . .

II. iii. 269. You should not haue the eminence of him,
But be as *Aiax.*

II. iii. 272.   *Vlis.* There is no tarrying here, the Hart <u>*Achilles*</u>
<u>Keepes thicket</u>: please it our Generall,
To call together all his <u>state of warre,</u>
Fresh Kings are come to *Troy*; to morrow
We must with all our <u>maine of power</u> stand fast:

Enter PANDARUS and a Seruant

III. i. 35.   *Ser.* with him the mortall *Venus*, <u>the heart bloud of beauty,</u>
<u>loues inuisible soule.</u>

Enter PARIS and HELENA

III. i. 47.   *Pan.* <u>Faire be to you my Lord,</u> and to all this faire company:
faire desires in all faire measure fairely guide them, especially
to you faire Queene, <u>faire thoughts be your faire pillow.</u>

III. i. 57.   *Par.* <u>*Nel*</u>, he is full of harmony.

III. i. 112.   *Pand.* Hee? no, sheele none of him, <u>they two are twaine.</u>

III. i. 127.   *Pan.*   *Loue, loue, nothing but loue, still more:*
For O loues Bow,
Shootes Bucke and Doe:
The Shaft confounds not that it wounds,
But tickles still the sore:
These Louers cry, oh ho they dye;
Yet that which seemes the wound to kill,
Doth turne oh ho, to ha ha he:
So dying loue liues still,
O ho a while, but ha ha ha,
O ho grones out for ha ha ha.—hey ho.

III. i. 168.   *Par.*   you shall doe more
Then all the <u>Iland Kings,</u> disarme great *Hector.*

III. i. 172.   *Hel.* Giues vs more <u>palme in beautie</u> then we haue:

Enter PANDARUS and TROYLUS Man

III. ii. 1.   *Pan.* How now, where's thy Maister, . . .

Enter TROYLUS

III. ii. 5.   *Pan.* O here he comes: How now, how now?

Troy. Sirra walke off.

Pan. Haue you seene my Cousin?

Troy. No *Pandarus*: I stalke about her doore
Like a strange soule vpon the Stigian bankes
Staying for waftage. O be thou my *Charon*,
And giue me swift transportance to those fields,
Where I may wallow in the Lilly beds
Propos'd for the deseruer. O gentle *Pandarus*,
From *Cupids* shoulder plucke his painted wings,
And flye with me to *Cressid*.

Pan. Walke here ith' Orchard, Ile bring her straight.

                                            Exit PANDARUS.

Troy. I am giddy; expectation whirles me round,
Th'imaginary relish is so sweete,
That it inchants my sence: what will it be
When that the watry pallats taste indeede
Loues thrice reputed Nectar? Death I feare me
* woon
Sounding distruction, or some ioy too fine,
Too subtile, potent, and too sharpe in sweetnesse,
For the capacitie of my ruder powers;
I feare it much, and I doe feare besides,
That I shall loose distinction in my ioyes,
As doth a battaile, when they charge on heapes
The enemy flying.   *Enter Pandarus.*

Pan. Shee's making her ready, sheele come straight; you must
be witty now, she does so blush, & fetches her winde so short, as
if she were fraid with a sprite: Ile fetch her; it is the prettiest
villaine, she fetches her breath so short as a new tane Sparrow.

                                            Exit Pand.

Troy. Euen such a passion doth imbrace my bosome:
My heart beates thicker then a feauorous pulse,
And all my powers doe their bestowing loose,
Like vassalage at vnawares encountring
The eye of Maiestie.

            Enter PANDARUS *and* CRESSIDA

* Keats's script.

III. ii. 47.   *Pan.* Come draw this curtaine, & let's see your picture.

.   .   .   .   .   .

III. ii. 51.   build there Carpenter, the ayre is sweete.

III. ii. 55.   *Troy.* You haue bereft me of all words Lady.

Pan. Words pay no debts; giue her deedes: but sheele bereaue you 'oth' deeds too, if shee call your actiuity in question: what billing againe? here's in witnesse whereof the Parties interchangeably. Come in, come in, Ile go get a fire?

Cres. Will you walke in my Lord?

Troy. O *Cressida,* how often haue I wisht me thus?

Cres. Wisht my Lord? the gods grant? O my Lord.

Troy. What should they grant? what makes this pretty abruption: what too curious dreg espies my sweete Lady in the fountaine of our loue?

III. ii. 125.   *Cres.* Hard to seeme won: but I was won my Lord

With the first glance; that euer pardon me,

If I confesse much you will play the tyrant:

I loue you now, but not till now so much

But I might maister it; infaith I lye:

My thoughts were like vnbrideled children grow

Too head-strong for their mother: see we fooles,

Why haue I blab'd: who shall be true to vs

When we are so vnsecret to our selues?

But though I lou'd you well, I woed you not,

And yet good faith I wisht my selfe a man;

Or that we women had mens priuiledge

Of speaking first. Sweet, bid me hold my tongue,

For in this rapture I shall surely speake

The thing I shall repent: see, see, your silence

Comming in dumbnesse, from my weakenesse drawes

My soule of counsell from me.

III. ii. 162.   *Cre.* To Angle for your thoughts:

III. ii. 174.   *Troy.* Of such a winnowed puriritie in loue:

How were I then vp-lifted! but alas,

I am as true, as truths simplicitie

And simpler then the infancie of truth.

III. ii. 192.   *Cres.* When time is old and hath forgot it selfe:
                    When water drops haue worne the Stones of *Troy*;
                    And blinde obliuion swallow'd Cities vp;
                    And mightie States characterlesse are grated
                    To dustie nothing;

III. ii. 215.   *Pan.* Whereupon I will shew you a Chamber, which bed,
                    because it shall not speake of your prettie encounters, presse it to
                    death: away.

     Enter VLYSSES, DIOMEDES, NESTOR, AGAMEMNON, MENELAUS
          and CHALCAS.   *Florish*

III. iii. 28.   *Cal.* And he shall buy my Daughter: and her presence,
                    Shall quite strike off all seruice I haue done,
                    In most accepted paine.

III. iii. 43.   *Vlis.* Why such vnplausiue eyes are bent? why turn'd on him?
                    If so, I haue derision medicinable,
                    To vse betweene your strangenesse and his pride,
                      .   .   .   .
III. iii. 48.   .   .   .   .   .   .   for supple knees,
                    Feede arrogance, and are the proud mans fees.

III. iii. 71.   *Patr.* They passe by strangely: they were vs'd to bend
                    To send their smiles before them to *Achilles*:
                    To come as humbly as they vs'd to creepe to holy Altars.
                       Achil. What am I poore of late?
                    Tis certaine, greatnesse once falne out with fortune,
                    Must fall out with men too: what the declin'd is,
                    He shall as soone reade in the eyes of others,
                    As feele in his owne fall: for men like butter-flies,
                    Shew not their mealie wings, but to the Summer:
                    And not a man for being simply man,
                    Hath any honour;

III. iii. 93.   *Achil.* Ile interrupt his reading: how now *Vlisses*?

III. iii. 107.   *Achil.*   but eye to eye oppos'd,
                    Salutes each other with each others forme,
                    For speculation turnes not to it selfe,

Till it hath trauail'd, and is married there
Where it may see it selfe:

III. iii. 120.   *Vlis.* . . . . . who like an arch reuerb'rate
The voyce againe; . . . .

III. iii. 134.   How some men creepe in skittish fortunes hall,
Whiles others play the Ideots in her eyes:
.   .   .   .   .   .

III. iii. 139.   They clap the lubber *Aiax* on the shoulder,

III. iii. 142.   *Achil.* For they past by me, as mysers doe by beggars,

III. iii. 145.   *Vlis.* Time hath (my Lord) a wallet at his backe,
Wherein he puts almes for obliuion:
A great siz'd monster of ingratitudes:
Those scraps are good deedes past,
Which are deuour'd as fast as they are made,
Forgot as soone as done: perseuerance, deere my Lord,
Keepes honor bright, to haue done, is to hang
Quite out of fashion, like a rustie male,
In monumentall mockrie: take the instant way,
For honour trauels in a straight so narrow,
Where one but goes a breast, keepe then the path:
For emulation hath a thousand Sonnes,
That one by one pursue; if you giue way,
Or hedge aside from the direct forth right;
Like to an entred Tyde, they all rush by,
And leaue you hindmost:
Or like a gallant Horse falne in first ranke,
Lye there for pauement to the abiect, ~~neere~~ rear *
Ore-run and trampled on: then what they doe in present,
Though lesse then yours in past, must ore-top yours:
For time is like a fashionable Hoste,
That slightly shakes his parting Guest by th' hand;
And with his armes out-stretcht, as he would flye,
Graspes in the commer: the welcome euer smiles,
And farewels goes out sighing: O let not vertue seeke
Remuneration for the thing it was: for beautie, wit,

* Keats's script.

High birth, vigor of bone, desert in seruice,

Loue, friendship, charity, are subiects all

To enuious and calumniating time:

One touch of nature makes the whole world kin:　　　|

That all with one consent praise new borne gaudes,

Though they are made and moulded of things past,

　　　* iv

And goe to dust, that is a little guilt,

More laud then guilt oredusted.　. . .

　　　　　　　　　sooner *

III. iii. 183.　Since things in motion begin to catch the eye,

Then what not stirs: . . . . . .

III. iii. 186.　If thou would'st not entombe thy selfe aliue,

And case thy reputation in thy Tent;

III. iii. 192.　　*Vlis.* The reasons are more potent and heroycall:

III. iii. 197.　　*Vlis.* The prouidence that's in a watchfull State,

Knowes almost euery graine of Plutoes gold;

Findes bottome in th' vncomprehensiue deepes;

Keepes place with thought; and almost like the gods,

| Doe thoughts vnuaile in their dumbe cradles:

III. iii. 223.　　*Patr.*　　　　　　　　and the weake wanton *Cupid*

Shall from your necke vnloose his amorous fould,

And like a dew drop from the Lyons mane,

† Be shooke to ayrie ayre.

III. iii. 231.　　*Patr.* Omission to doe what is necessary,

Seales a commission to a blanke of danger,

And danger like an ague subtly taints

Euen then when we sit idely in the sunne.

III. iii. 238.　　*Achil.*　　　　　　　I haue a womans longing,

An appetite that I am sicke withall,

To see great *Hector* in his weedes of peace;　　　*Enter Thersi.*

　　　　　　　　　* Keats's script.

KEATS'S NOTE] † Where fore should this ayrie be left out?

<u>To talke with him, and to behold his visage,</u>
<u>Euen to my full of view.</u> A labour sau'd.

III. iii. 248.   *Ther.* He must fight singly to morrow with *Hector*, and is so <u>prophetically</u> proud of an heroicall cudgelling, that he raues in saying nothing.

III. iii. 272.   *Ther.*   <u>he professes notanswering;</u>

III. iii. 314.   *Achil.* <u>My minde is troubled like a Fountaine stir'd,</u>
<u>And I my selfe see not the bottome of it.</u>

Enter at one doore ÆNEAS with a Torch, at another PARIS, DIEPHOEBUS,
ANTHENOR, DIOMED *the Grecian, with Torches*

IV. i. 17.   │   *Diom.* By *Ioue*, Ile play the hunter for thy life,
│   With all my force, pursuite and pollicy.   [Semi-colon in-
│   *Æne.* And thou shalt hunt a Lyon that will flye   serted for com-
│   With his face backward; <u>in humaine gentlenesse</u>‡   ma in mid-line,
│   Welcome to Troy;   and colon at
                                   end deleted by
                                   Keats.]

IV. i. 27.   *Diom.* <u>A thousand compleate courses of the Sunne,</u>

IV. i. 48.   *Par.* The <u>bitter disposition of the time will haue it so.</u>

IV. i. 51.   *Par.* And tell me noble *Diomed*; faith tell me true,
<u>Euen in the soule of sound good fellowship,</u>
Who in your thoughts merits faire *Helen* most?
My selfe, or *Menelaus*?
     Diom. Both alike.
He merits well to haue her, that doth seeke her,
Not making any scruple of her soylure,
With such a hell of paine, and world of charge.
And you as well to keepe her, that defend her,
Not pallating the taste of her dishonour,
With such a costly losse of wealth and friends:
He like a puling Cuckold, would drinke vp
The lees and dregs of a flat tamed peece:
You like a letcher, out of whorish loynes,
Are pleas'd to breede out your inheritors:
Both merits poyz'd, each weighs no lesse nor more,
But he as he, which heauier for a whore.

IV. i. 69. *Dio*. For euery false drop in her baudy veines,
A Grecians life hath sunke: . . . .

IV. i. 72. . . . . Since she could speake,
She hath not giuen so many good words breath,
As for her, Greekes and Troians suffred death.

Enter TROYLUS *and* CRESSIDA

IV. ii. 1. *Troy*. Deere trouble not your selfe: the morne is cold.

IV. ii. 4. *Troy*. To bed, to bed: sleepe kill those pritty eyes,
And giue as soft attachment to thy sences,
As Infants empty of all thought.

IV. ii. 8. *Troy*. O *Cressida*! but that the busie day ‖
Wak't by the Larke, hath rouz'd the ribauld Crowes,
And dreaming night will hide our eyes no longer:
I would not from thee.

IV. ii. 15. *Troy*. You will catch cold, and curse me.

IV. ii. 18. *Cres*.   Harke, ther's one vp?

IV. ii. 73. *Troy*.   and my Lord *Æneas*,
We met by chance; you did not finde me here.

IV. ii. 103. *Cres*. I will not Vnckle: I haue forgot my Father:
I know no touch of consanguinitie:
No kin, no loue, no bloud, no soule, so neere me,
As the sweet *Troylus*:

Enter PARIS, TROYLUS, ÆNEAS, DEIPHEBUS, ANTHENOR *and* DIOMEDES

IV. iii. 1. *Par*. It is great morning,   ‖

Enter PANDARUS *and* CRESSID

IV. iv. 2. *Cres*. Why tell you me of moderation?
The griefe is fine, full perfect that I taste,
And no lesse in a sense as strong
As that which causeth it. How can I moderate it?
If I could temporise with my affection,

Or brew it to a weake and colder pallat,
The like alaiment could I giue my griefe:
My loue admits no qualifying crosse;   *Enter Troylus.*
No more my griefe, in such a precious losse.

IV. iv. 24.   *Troy. Cressid*: I loue thee in so strange a puritie;
That the blest gods, as angry with my fancie,
More bright in zeale, then the deuotion which
Cold lips blow to their Deities: take thee from me.

IV. iv. 33.   *Troy.* And sodainely, where iniurie of chance
Puts backe leaue-taking, iustles roughly by
All time of pause; rudely beguiles our lips
Of all reioyndure: forcibly preuents
Our lockt embrasures; strangles our deare vowes,
Euen in the birth of our owne laboring breath.
We two, that with so many thousand sighes
Did buy each other, must poorely sell our selues,
With the rude breuitie and discharge of our ne.*
[Semi-colon Iniurious time; now with a robbers haste
deleted by
Keats.]   Crams his rich theeuerie vp, he knowes not how.
As many farwels as be stars in heauen,
With distinct breath, and consign'd kisses to them,
He fumbles vp into a loose adiew;
And scants vs with a single famisht kisse,
Distasting with the salt of broken teares.   *Enter Æneas.*

IV. iv. 60.   *Troy.* Nay, we must vse expostulation kindely,
For it is parting from vs:
I speake not, be thou true, as fearing thee:
For I will throw my Gloue to death himselfe,
That there's no maculation in thy heart:
But be thou true, say I, to fashion in
My sequent protestation:

IV. iv. 84.   *Troy.* In this I doe not call your faith in question
So mainely as my merit: . . . .

. . . .

* Keats's script.

IV. iv. 89.   But I can tell that in each grace of these,
               There lurkes a still and dumb-discoursiue diuell,

IV. iv. 96.   *Troy*. When we will tempt the frailtie of our powers,
               Presuming on their changefull potencie.

IV. iv. 102.   *Troy*. Who I? alas it is my vice, my fault:
               Whiles others fish with craft for great opinion,
               I, with great truth, catch meere simplicitie;

IV. iv. 113.   *Troy*.   and by my soule, faire **Greeke**,
               If ere thou stand at mercy of my Sword,
               Name *Cressid*, and thy life shall be as safe
               As *Priam* is in Illion?

IV. iv. 123.   *Troy*.   I tell thee Lord of Greece:
               Shee is as farre high soaring o're thy praises,
               As thou vnworthy to be cal'd her seruant:
               I charge thee vse her well, euen for my charge:
               For by the dreadfull *Pluto*, if thou do'st not,
               (Though the great bulke *Achilles* be thy guard)
               Ile cut thy throate.

               Enter AIAX *armed*, ACHILLES, PATROCLUS, AGAMEMNON, MENELAUS,
                       VLISSES, NESTOR, CALCAS &c.

IV. v. 3.   *Aga*. Giue with thy Trumpet a loud note to **Troy**
               Thou dreadful *Aiax*, that the appauled aire
               May pierce the head of the great Combatant,
               And hale him hither.
                 Aia. Thou, Trumpet, ther's my purse;
               Now cracke thy lungs, and split thy brasen pipe:
               Blow villaine, till thy sphered Bias cheeke
               Out-swell the collicke of puft *Aquilon*:
               Come, stretch thy chest, and let thy eyes spout bloud:
               Thou blowest for *Hector*.
                 Vlis. No Trumpet answers.
                 Achil. 'Tis but early dayes.
                 Aga. Is not yong *Diomed* with *Calcas* daughter?
                 Vlis. 'Tis he, I ken the manner of his gate,
               He rises on the toe: that spirit of his
               In aspiration lifts him from the earth.

IV. v. 24.   *Achil.* Ile take that winter from your lips faire Lady

IV. v. 54.   *Vlis.* Fie, fie, vpon her:
                 Ther 's a language in her eye, her cheeke, her lip;
                 Nay, her foote speakes, her wanton spirites looke out
                                    on *
                 At euery ioynt, and motiue of her body:
                 Oh these encounterers so glib of tongue, |
                                         r *
                 That giue a coasting welcome e⁄e it comes;
                 And wide vnclaspe the tables of their thoughts,
                 To euery tickling reader: set them downe,
                 For sluttish spoyles of opportunitie;
                 And daughters of the game.

IV. v. 67.   *Æne.*   will you the Knights
                 Shall to the edge of all extremitie
                 Pursue each other; or shall be diuided
                 By any voyce, or order of the field: *Hector* bad aske?

IV. v. 79.   *Æne.* Valour and pride excell themselues in *Hector*;
                 The one almost as infinite as all;
                 The other blanke as nothing: weigh him well:
                 And that which lookes like pride, is curtesie:

IV. v. 95.   *Aga.* What Troian is that same that lookes so heauy?
                 Vlis. The yongest Sonne of *Priam*;
                 A true Knight; they call him *Troylus*;
                 Not yet mature, yet matchlesse, firme of word,
                 Speaking in deedes, and deedelesse in his tongue;
                 Not soone prouok't, nor being prouok't, soone calm'd;
                 His heart and hand both open, and both free:
                 For what he has, he giues; what thinkes, he shewes;
                 Yet giues he not till iudgement guide his bounty,
                 Nor dignifies an impaire thought with breath:
                 Manly as *Hector*, but more dangerous;
                 For *Hector* in his blaze of wrath subscribes
                 To tender obiects; but he, in heate of action,
                 Is more vindecatiue then iealous loue,
                 They call him *Troylus*; and on him erect,

                          * Keats's script.

A second hope, as fairely built as *Hector*.
Thus saies *Æneas*, one that knowes the youth,
Euen to his inches: and with priuate soule,
Did in great Illion thus translate him to me.

IV. v. 126.   *Hect.*   my Mothers bloud
Runs on the dexter cheeke, and this sinister
Bounds in my fathers:

IV. v. 137.   *Aia.* I thanke thee *Hector*:
Thou art too gentle, and too free a man:
I came to kill thee Cozen, and beare hence
A great addition, earned in thy death.

IV. v. 165.   *Aga.* What 's past, and what 's to come, is strew'd with huskes,
And formelesse ruine of obliuion:

IV. v. 181.   *Hect.* O pardon, I offend.

IV. v. 184.   *Nest.*   and I haue seen thee
As hot as *Perseus*, spurre thy Phrygian Steed,
And seene thee scorning forfeits and subduments,
When thou hast hung thy aduanced sword i' th' ayre,
Not letting it decline, on the declined:
That I haue said vnto my standers by,
Loe Iupiter is yonder, dealing life.
And I haue seene thee pause, and take thy breath,
When that a ring of Greekes haue hem'd thee in,
Like an Olympian wrestling. This haue I seene,
But this thy countenance (still lockt in steele)
I neuer saw till now.

IV. v. 200.   *Æne.* 'Tis the old *Nestor*.
    Hect. Let me embrace thee good old Chronicle,
That hast so long walk'd hand in hand with time;
Most reuerend *Nestor*, I am glad to claspe thee.

IV. v. 206.   *Hect.* I would they could.
    Nest. Ha? by this white beard I'ld fight with thee to morrow.
Well, welcom, welcome: I haue seen the time.

IV. v. 212.   *Hect.* I know your fauour Lord *Vlysses* well.
Ah sir, there 's many a Greeke and Troyan dead,
Since first I saw your selfe, and *Diomed*
In Illion, on your Greekish Embassie.

IV. v. 219.   *Vlys.* Yond Towers, whose wanton tops do busse the clouds,
Must kisse their owne feet.
    Hect. I must not beleeue you:
There they stand yet: and modestly I thinke,
The fall of euery Phrygian stone will cost
A drop of Grecian blood: the end crownes all,
And that old common Arbitrator, Time,
Will one day end it.

IV. v. 227.   *Vlys.* After the Generall, I beseech you next
To Feast with me, and see me at my Tent.
    Achil. I shall forestall thee Lord *Vlysses*, thou:
Now *Hector* I haue fed mine eyes on thee,
I haue with exact view perus'd thee *Hector*,
And quoted ioynt by ioynt.
    Hect. Is this *Achilles* ?
    Achil. I am *Achilles*.
    Hect. Stand faire I prythee, let me looke on thee.
    Achil. Behold thy fill.
    Hect. Nay, I haue done already.
    Achil. Thou art to breefe, I will the second time,
As I would buy thee, view thee, limbe by limbe.
    Hect. O like a Booke of sport thou'lt reade me ore:
But there 's more in me then thou vnderstand'st.
Why doest thou so oppresse me with thine eye ?
    Achil. Tell me you Heauens, in which part of his body
Shall I destroy him ? Whether there, or there, or there,
That I may giue the locall wound a name,
And make distinct the very breach, where-out
Hectors great spirit flaw. Answer me heauens.
    Hect. It would discredit the blest Gods, proud man,
To answer such a question: Stand againe;
Think'st thou to catch my life so pleasantly,
As to prenominate in nice coniecture
Where thou wilt hit me dead ?

Achil. I tell thee yea.

Hect. Wert thou the Oracle to tell me so,
I'ld not beleeue thee: henceforth guard thee well,
For Ile not kill thee there, nor there, nor there,
But by the forge that stythied Mars his helme,
Ile kill thee euery where, yea, ore and ore.
You wisest Grecians, pardon me this bragge,
His insolence drawes folly from my lips,
But Ile endeuour deeds to match these words,
Or may I neuer——

Enter ACHILLES, *and* PATROCLUS

V. i. 1.   *Achil.* Ile heat his blood with Greekish wine to night
Which with my Cemitar Ile coole to morrow:

V. i. 41.   *Ther.* Finch Egge.

V. i. 56.   *Ther.* Heere's *Agamemnon,* an honest fellow enough, and one
that loues Quailes, but he has not so much Braine as eare-wax;

.   .   .   .

V. i. 61.   .   .   .   .   .   .   oblique memoriall of Cuckolds,

Enter DIOMED

.   .   .

Enter TROYLUS *and* VLISSES

Vlis. Stand where the Torch may not discouer vs.

Enter CRESSID

V. ii. 74.   *Cres.* O all you gods! O prettie, prettie pledge;
Thy Maister now lies thinking in his bed
Of thee and me, and sighes, and takes my Gloue,
And giues memoriall daintie kisses to it;
As I kisse thee.

V. ii. 106.   *Cres.* Ah poore our sexe; this fault in vs I finde:
The errour of our eye, directs our minde.

V. ii. 112.   *Vlis.* Why stay we then?
Troy. To make a recordation to my soule
Of euery syllable that here was spoke:

V. ii. 126.   *Troy*. Let it not be beleeu'd for womanhood:
                Thinke we had mothers; doe not giue aduantage
                To stubborne Criticks, apt without a theame
                For deprauation, to square the generall sex
                By *Cressids* rule. Rather thinke this not *Cressid*.

V. ii. 143.   *Troy*.   This is, and is not *Cressid*:
                Within my soule, there doth conduce a fight
                Of this strange nature, that a thing inseperate,
                Diuides more wider then the skie and earth:
                And yet the spacious bredth of this diuision,
                Admits no Orifex for a point as subtle,
                As *Ariachnes* broken woofe to enter:

V. ii. 162.   *Troy*.   neuer did yong man fancy
                With so eternall, and so fixt a soule.

V. ii. 168.   *Troy*.   Not the dreadfull spout,
                Which Shipmen doe the Hurricano call,
                Constring'd in masse by the almighty Fenne,
                Shall dizzie with more clamour Neptunes eare
                In his discent; then shall my prompted sword
                Falling on *Diomed*.

V. ii. 191.   *Ther*. the Parrot will not doe more for an Almond, then I
                for a commodious drab:

                Enter HECTOR *and* ANDROMACHE

V. iii. 10.   *And*.   for I haue dreampt
                Of bloudy turbulence; and this whole night
                Hath nothing beene but shapes, and formes of slaughter.

V. iii. 13.   *Hect*. Ho? bid my Trumpet sound.
                Cass. No notes of sallie, for the heauens, sweet brother.

V. iii. 16.   *Cass*. The gods are deafe to hot and peeuish vowes;
                They are polluted offrings, more abhord
                Then spotted Liuers in the sacrifice.

V. iii. 32. | *Hect*. I am to day ith' vaine of Chiualrie:

V. iii. 37. | *Troy.* Brother, you haue a vice of mercy in you;
| Which better fits a Lyon, then a man.

V. iii. 41. *Troy.* Euen in the fanne and winde of your fair Sword:

V. iii. 44. *Troy.* For th' loue of all the gods
Let's leaue the Hermit Pitty with our Mothers;

V. iii. 52. *Troy.* Not fate, obedience, nor the hand of *Mars,*
Beckning with fierie trunchion my retire;

V. iii. 85. *Cass.* Behold distraction, frenzie, and amazement,
Like witlesse Antickes one another meete,

Enter AGAMEMNON

V. v. 7. *Aga.*   bastard *Margarelon*
Hath *Doreus* prisoner.
And stands Calossus-wise wauing his beame,

Enter HECTOR

.   .   .

Enter ACHILLES *and his Myrmidons*

V. viii. 5. *Achil.* Looke *Hector* how the Sunne begins to set;
How vgly night comes breathing at his heeles,
Euen with the vaile and darking of the Sunne.

Enter PANDARUS

V. x. 42. *Pan.* Full merrily the humble Bee doth sing,
Till he hath lost his hony, and his sting.

V. x. 52. Brethren and sisters of the hold-dore trade, |